POP MUSIC & MORALITY

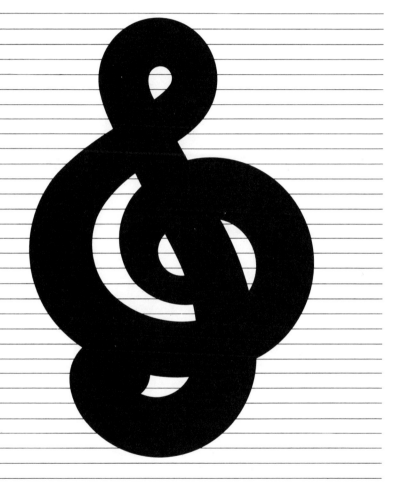

LEX DE AZEVEDO
with Chris Conkling

Embryo Books · North Hollywood, California, 1982

Lithographed in the United States of America

Publishers Press
Salt Lake City, Utah

Dedication

To my seven children: Carrie, Julie, Emilie, Alexis, Rachel, Rebecca, and Christian. May they always discern between good and evil, and spend their lives in pursuit of beauty and truth.

Acknowledgements

As a composer, I find that my thoughts tend to seek musical rather than literary expression. I would like to thank co-author Chris Conkling and editor Mel Leavitt for helping translate those thoughts into words. I would also like to thank researcher Lynn Aaron for her enthusiasm for this project; my mother, Alyce King Clarke, for giving me life and a love of the "hot notes"; my wife, Linda, for maintaining a peaceful, orderly home without which I could not create, and above all, my Father in Heaven for sending me down in the Saturday of time in the heat of the battle.

Contents

Introduction

Music moves us, and we know not why; we feel the tears, but cannot trace their source. Is it the language of some other state, born of memory? For what can wake the soul's strong instinct of another world like music?

L.E. Landon

Talk about a no-win situation!

I had been asked to speak at a stake fireside on the subject of rock music and morality, a highly controversial topic at best. I was soon to find out the evening's presentation would be more controversial than usual because a member of the stake presidency had closed down a youth dance the night before. In his judgment, the music and the kids had gotten out of hand.

I could feel the emotional intensity in the air as the kids filed in to sit on one side of the chapel and the adults sat on the other. The audience did not want to hear a lecture; they wanted to air their grievances about last night's blow-up. To help them let off steam, I opened the meeting to a discussion of the dance. That was when the lid came flying off the pressure cooker. I was bombarded by questions and comments from both sides:

"Why is the Church always against new music? It was even against the waltz when it first came out."

"I am sure the Lord is displeased when our youth dance to that loud, vulgar music in his own house."

"You think it's loud and vulgar because you don't like it. Your parents probably thought *your* music was loud and vulgar."

"Why don't you kids learn to appreciate *real* music—classical music—instead of idolizing those immoral rock stars."

"You think rock singers are immoral? Did you ever read about Wagner or Liszt?"

"But that's different. Their music was beautiful and uplifting. It was good."

"*Boring* might be a better word for it!"

One elderly brother stood to settle the whole matter. "I can't always make out the words, but whenever I hear the sound of that electric gee-tar I know they're singing about dope!" And with that he threw himself back down into his seat as if he had solved every issue of the evening once and for all.

A few nodded in agreement. Most snickered or laughed out loud. I was tempted to chuckle myself until I realized that he had made the most profound comment of the evening. He was literally right. To *him*, every song with an electric "gee-tar" *was* associated with dope. In his mind and memory, the electric "gee-tar" and dope were inextricably connected.

In each of our minds, certain kinds of music are tied deeply to our own personal experiences and emotions. Our favorite music has an intensely personal meaning to us. Memories of childhood, first date, first love, youth conferences, prom night, that special testimony meeting, marriage, and old friends may all be tied to a certain kind of music in one way or another. Thus, when someone attacks our music, they may also be attacking our deepest, most personal experiences. It is as if they were attacking our very identity.

Because our response to music is so intensely personal, it is difficult to be objective about it. Most discussions about music and morality fail to focus on the moral issues and degenerate into arguments about personal tastes. We tend to confuse moral judgments with personal preferences, to ascribe moral qualities to things we like. In short, that which we like we call "good," and that which we don't like we call "bad."

Parents and leaders of youth would do well not to point the finger at broad categories, such as "hard rock," "soft rock," or "country and western" for three reasons: (1) Categories are vague and mean different things to different people; (2) Every category contains both good and bad music; and, (3) To discuss categories is to miss the entire point. Moral and immoral songs exist in every kind of music, and attacking a specific category may lead a person to feel justified in listening to equally immoral music in another category.

My purpose in writing this book is to give both youth and adults tools to judge the moral impact of any music. Hopefully, this will help strengthen us all while avoiding the unnecessary alienation of our young people.

My earliest memories involve music, and I have been studying and creating music almost all my life. And yet, the more I learn the less I understand music's magical grasp on the human soul. I know what music can do, but I do not fully understand how it does it. What is the charm of a melody? Why the emotional response to a progression of harmonies? Wherein lies the magnetism of an infectious rhythm? I have spent my life chasing notes, trying to unravel their hidden mysteries, and yet I still stand in awe of music's strange powers.

In writing this book, I want to share some of my personal experiences with music, and then explore music's incredible power, consider the moral issues raised by that power, and look at the music of today in light of its moral consequences.

Beethoven said that "music is the mediator between the spiritual and the sensual life." It can lead us either way. Music can greatly degrade or greatly ennoble our lives. Once we

understand what it can do for us, we will be able to use that
musical power more wisely.

PART ONE

Reflections of a Mormon in the Music Business

*All musical people
seem to be happy; it is to them
the engrossing pursuit;
almost the only innocent and
unpunished passion.*

Sydney Smith

U ntil I met my wife I had only three great loves—the gospel, music, and my piano. My mother was Alyce King, one of the four singing King Sisters. I was born in 1943 during the height of the big band era while my mother and her sisters were singing across the country. I suppose I am one of the first Mormons to have the dubious honor of being born, almost literally, backstage.

My earliest memories are of music. As a child, I remember sitting underneath the piano for hours, listening to my mother and her sisters rehearse. I can recall being transported by the beautiful harmonies. Sometimes a particular chord would excite me so much that I would grab my mother's leg, hug it, and beg, "Sing that part again!" When I was five years old, I accidentally discovered a beautiful chord and was so thrilled that I leaned over and kissed the piano keys. From that age on, my life has been immersed in music, from the works of the great masters to jazz and pop.

My father, Sydney de Azevedo, was serving overseas in the Army during my first five years, and he died when I was only ten. In his stead, my grandfather, William King Driggs, became the father figure in my life. It was he, along with my mother, who taught me to love the gospel and who helped me grow spiritually.

William King Driggs was a fascinating man. He grew up

in Pleasant Grove, Utah, and was president of his BYU class in 1907. He spent his life as a music teacher, travelling through Utah and Colorado, Idaho and California, giving piano lessons, writing operas for towns of less than 500 people, and doing whatever else it took to keep body and soul together. He raised eight children, formed a family orchestra, and went from town to town giving concerts, passing the hat and trying to keep his car from being repossessed.

My mother lived in a different city each year of her childhood. Grandfather never owned a home. Such things as real estate and money were trivial to him, much to the chagrin of his wife and children. As the saying goes, he gave his family everything money could not buy: an intense passion for the gospel, for the arts, for family and children, and especially for music.

Among my earliest memories are those of sitting on Grandpa's thin lap as he told me of the Prophet Joseph Smith, and of his own grandfather, Parley P. Pratt, one of the original twelve apostles and author of several of our hymns, and of the sacrifices and adventures of the Saints crossing the plains. His stories enthralled me. I think I was first touched by the Spirit while sitting on his knee. I was extremely blessed, because my life always had a focus. From my youngest days I knew two things: The gospel was true and music would be my life.

In fact, these two great passions so possessed me that I sometimes wondered if they would ever come into conflict. Would I ever have to sacrifice music for the gospel, or the gospel for music? Would I ever have to choose between them? Not knowing the answer, I continued to try to grow in both areas.

Throughout junior and senior high school I kept up my musical training and also had my own dance bands. After graduation from North Hollywood High, I went to BYU for a semester, but at that time it did not seem to offer the kind of training I needed, so I transferred back to USC and continued my studies there. Going to school in Los Angeles enabled me to travel with the King Sisters as their arranger and accompanist and to meet many influential people in the music business through them.

One summer while working with the King Sisters in Lake Tahoe, I met the Four Preps, a popular quartet in the early sixties. One of them was a Latter-day Saint (Glen Larson, now a successful television producer), and they hired me as their musical director. It was exciting to spend my weekends and holidays flying around the country in a private plane, doing college concerts, and I appreciated being able to make a good living while continuing my college education.

At the time I planned to become a concert pianist. So with the help of my parents and the bank, I bought a seven thousand-dollar Steinway grand piano. The Steinway is the Cadillac of pianos, and mine was the most beautiful in the world. It had a black satin finish with gold leaf and red velvet inside. Its tone was magnificent. I would practice six or seven hours a day, sinking my fingers into the pearl-white ivories. I loved that piano. My idea of a good date was to invite a girl over to listen to me practice all evening (and if she got bored, that was the last time I asked her out). That piano became my first love—I almost worshipped it.

It was just at this point that my bishop, Gerald Plumb, asked me if I would accept a mission call. Deep down I knew I should go, but to a nineteen-year old, two and a half years is a long time. Would I ever be able to make up for all that lost practice time? Could I survive a two and a half year separation from my beloved Steinway? I told the bishop I would pray about it.

This was the most difficult decision of my life. I was torn

between two loves. I knew the scripture, "where your treasure is, there will your heart be also," and wondered if I was investing too much in my piano and my career.

During this time of decision, I dreamed one night that I was in the hereafter. I looked up into the celestial kingdom and saw my Steinway piano. I was looking *up* because I was not there. My Steinway had filled the measure of its creation, but I had not! For a moment I was able to grasp the eternal perspective of life. If I would put the Lord's work first, I would have the eternities to practice my beloved Steinway. Otherwise, we might be separated.

Other thoughts flooded my mind. Should I bet two and a half years of practice time against the eternities? And what guarantees of success did I have even if I did stay home? I could lose my arm. I could die young like Shubert or Mozart or my father. And when I contemplated the kind of music there might be in the celestial kingdom, I began to realize how little I could learn about music in this life anyway. What will music sound like when played on celestial instruments and sung by celestial voices? I realized that I would be risking everything to gain almost nothing. It was a bad bet. I told my bishop I would go.

When I said goodby to my beloved Steinway in the spring of 1962, I thought I was making the greatest sacrifice since Abraham. As it turned out, I became one of the last missionaries to enter Brazil without going through the language training center, one of the last missionaries to serve for two and a half years. In short, I was one of the last of the *real* missionaries!

In my dream, I had seen a glimpse of the eternal perspective. My years in Brazil enlarged that perspective. Those two and a half years would serve as a standard by which I made all future decisions. The self-discipline, concentration, and consistency I developed on my mission more than made up for the thirty months of lost practice. I came to understand the Lord's promise to his faithful in the first Psalm:

> *Blessed is the man that walketh not in the counsel of the ungodly...*
> *And he shall be like a tree planted by the rivers of water, that bringeth forth his fruit in his season; his leaf also shall not wither; and whatsoever he doeth shall prosper. (Ps. 1:1, 3)*

This scripture explaines why some greatly talented people never seem to prosper. Caught up in their own personal disasters—divorces, drugs, alcohol, the inability to get along with others—they stumble along, while many consistent, disciplined people make steady progress.

Furthermore, during that time I came to realize that for me the cost of becoming a concert pianist (the hours of practice, the time spent touring away from my family) was too great. Had I stayed home, I might have spent those two and a half years and many more striving to attain something I actually didn't want. As Elder Boyd K. Packer has said, "There are many who struggle and climb and finally reach the top of the ladder, only to find that it is leaning against the wrong wall."[1]

While I was on my mission, two musical events occurred which would dramatically affect my personal life and the entire direction of my career. First, my family was signed by ABC to perform on a weekly musical television program called "The King Family Show." But even more importantly, an English musical group called the Beatles became world famous and changed the face of popular music forever.

I returned home in the fall of 1965. A family friend, Karl Engemann, an executive at Capitol Records, offered me a job as a record producer. A record producer in pop music does many things. He discovers new talent, chooses songs, produces album covers, creates the artist's image, oversees musical arrangements, and supervises recording sessions.

Although I thought I knew quite a bit about pop music, I had been entirely out of the music scene for two and a half years. When I left for Brazil, there were basically two types of pop music. One featured the moon/spoon/croon tunes— slow, gentle love songs such as those sung by Johnny Mathis. The other consisted of upbeat novelty tunes such as "Rockin' Robin," "Poison Ivy," and "Splish Splash." I was still unaware that a revolution had occurred in pop music.

One of my first assignments for Capitol Records was to investigate a "new" kind of music coming out of San Francisco. It was associated with the word *psychedelic*, and was performed by groups with strange names like The Jefferson Airplane, Quicksilver Messenger Service, Country Joe and the Fish, Moby Grape, and The Grateful Dead. Capitol sent me to San Francisco to see several such groups perform at the Fillmore Auditorium.

My wife, Linda, and I had just married and we thought it would be fun to make the trip together. We got out of our car about a block from the auditorium. Linda was wearing a nice dress. I was still wearing my missionary tracting shoes, white shirt, and narrow tie. As we approached the auditorium, the pavement started to vibrate beneath our feet. Once inside, we couldn't believe what we were seeing and hearing.

The music was so loud we couldn't even hear it ... we just felt it! Everyone was dressed in what appeared to us to be bizarre costumes. The smell of marijuana enveloped us. Kids danced in the strobe lights, flickering like slow-motion Charlie Chaplins. The walls were filled with huge pulsating oil projections that looked like giant amoebas multiplying and dividing in four-four time.

I tried to stay calm. My mission president had warned me not to go home cursing the wicked world like some missionaries do. I tried not to overreact, but the culture shock was too great. I stood there in my white shirt and tie and said to myself, "This is hell. I have stumbled into Sodom and Gomorrah." I couldn't believe the changes that had taken place during my mission years.

The next few months made a believer of me. I had always thought that pop music, though often insipid, was at least harmless, but that was no longer the case. The acid rock of the mid-sixties convinced me that music could be a powerful promoter of sex, drugs, and revolution. I was amazed at how quickly the record producers fell over each other to sign these groups up!

As social values deteriorated and record companies increasingly became advocates of the new morality, I knew that I would eventually have to get out of the record business. Other Latter-day Saints in the business sensed the same thing.

Before I finally got out, however, I had a few interesting experiences. I produced a hit comedy record with Mrs. Miller, an elderly woman whose incredible vibrato gave a unique interpretation to several current hit tunes. I also produced a number-one record with a bubble-gum rock group called the Human Be-inz. The making of this record resulted in two baptisms and taught me some disillusioning truths about how a hit is made.

Tom Shannonburger, Capitol's promotion man in Cleveland, called me one day to say he had found a local group with all the makings of another Beatles. He guaranteed that if I would record them, he would make sure that they became number one in the Cleveland area. I flew to Cleveland and listened to the group. Once we got them to turn their amplifiers down and heard them at a reasonable level, I realized that their poor material was exceeded only by their poor musicianship. Still, we decided to record their only song with any commercial potential, an old Isley Brothers hit called "Nobody But Me."

As we started recording, however, we found ourselves faced with a very serious problem: the drummer could not keep time. We let the other musicians take a break, hooked up a metronome to the drummer's headset, counted the number of beats in the song, and had him play by himself. Six hours later, we had two and a half minutes of drum on tape!

And so it went as each instrument was laboriously added to the track. We spent hours tuning guitars, trying to get the right fill in the right place, and erasing mistakes. Each musician played the same passage many times, trying to get it right. We spent two days recording the lead singer. As no one else in the group could sing very well, he and I overdubbed our voices six times for the backup parts. No one played the keyboards, so I overdubbed several piano tracks and an organ track. The rhythm still wasn't strong enough, so we beat on pop bottles, chains, tambourines, and anything else we could find in the studio to make a noise.

Two hundred and fifty studio hours later, we finished the track. To everyone's amazement, it sounded like a hit. We quickly wrote and recorded a tune for the back side, and I headed home to Los Angeles to make peace with my wife after a month's absence.

Tom Shannonburger kept his promise and promoted the song until it became the best-selling record in Cleveland. It gradually appeared on other local charts around the country and, in February of 1968, "Nobody But Me" by the Human Beinz became the number one record in the nation. It's amazing what you can do with very little talent and two hundred and fifty hours of studio time.

Then the worst news of all came. Karl Engemann called and said, "Lex, the record is doing great. We need an album. Can you go back to Cleveland and cut nine more tunes?"

Much to my wife's chagrin, I went back to Cleveland for several months. Not only did we cut a hit album, but Tom Shannonburger, the cigar-smoking, tough-talking record promotion man and his wife both became Latter-day Saints.

About this time I decided to quit Capitol Records. It was apparent that the record business would continue its downward path. As an elders quorum president, I didn't feel comfortable spending three evenings a week in nightclubs looking for new talent. And how could I, in good conscience, make my living producing groups who promoted sex, drugs, and violence? The scriptures about serving two masters became tremendously real to me.

Moreover, I was simply not happy. I really wanted to compose, orchestrate, and conduct music, and there was little time left for that while producing records. So, in 1968 I finally left Capitol to try to make a living as a freelance arranger and composer.

It was difficult to leave the security of a steady job for the uncertainties of freelancing. Many times we didn't know where our next month's house payment would come from, but we gained a strong testimony of tithing and somehow we always managed.

I left Capitol feeling that I would have more control over my life and my work. But that wasn't always the case. In 1970 I composed the score for a film called *Beautiful People*. When it bombed, the producers spiced it up with an abundance of nude scenes and released it as an R-rated film that probably should have been X-rated. Ironically, the first place it opened was in Salt Lake City—where else? I was a very embarrassed seminary teacher.

A few years later I was hired as an arranger and rehearsal pianist for *The Sonny and Cher Comedy Hour* on CBS, and found myself in a smoke-filled rehearsal hall, surrounded by that interesting assortment of people who grind out Hollywood's weekly television shows. The daily fare consisted of clever repartee, sexual innuendos, and fast jokes. The conversations always centered around the latest trends in hair, clothes, restaurants, imported water, and movies. Although I never really preached to these people, everyone knew I was a Mormon. (Perhaps it was the white shirt and narrow tie I still wore.) Sometimes when I was sitting at the piano, Sonny would say, "Okay Mormon, play!"

In that company I felt a little uncomfortable, even inferior, as my "comebacks" were too slow and clean to impress anyone. In this group I was the odd man out—the square piano player in the corner trying not to laugh at the jokes. This was life in Hollywood's fast lane, and I was peddling a mo-ped on the soft shoulder!

I generally kept to myself, but was friendly to those who dared be seen talking with me in public. As the season progressed, however, an interesting change occurred. Although I was still the oddball to the group as a whole, people would seek me out individually when they had tired of the surface banter and wanted genuine conversation. We usually began by talking about why I was so different and ended up discussing the gospel.

One day Sonny Bono asked me to have lunch with him. He asked me about the Church, and I told him about the Book of Mormon and the restoration of the gospel. "You know, that's really beautiful," he said. "I could never believe that myself, but I wish I could. I really wish I could."

With time, my feelings toward these people changed. As

we became friends, I saw that behind the facade of clever repartee and trendy lifestyles were lonely, insecure children of our Father in Heaven, many of them desperately looking for some meaning in life. My feelings of inferiority and alienation were replaced with feelings of genuine love and compassion as I realized how blessed I was to have a loving family, a purpose in life and an abundance of real friends. I no longer felt alone.

That feeling comforted me, but did not make my work any easier. I had left the recording business in order to gain more control over my working environment. Now I found myself caught in the midst of the same environment, but working twice as hard. Few can imagine what it takes to grind out a weekly musical variety show. During the television season, my week went typically like this:

Monday and Tuesday were spent working with the choreographer, putting together introductions and musical cues. On Tuesday night, I began the orchestration, often working through the night, handing off score sheet after score sheet to the copyists, whose job it was to extract each instrument line and copy it individually. Quite often, I left the office just in time to get to the recording studio and begin conducting the orchestra at 8:00 a.m. Wednesday morning.

Already exhausted from the night's work and the pressure to conduct efficiently (each minute cost hundreds of dollars), I was often called upon to revise the score during a ten-minute orchestra break, to satisfy a producer or director. The recording session usually ended at midnight. At three or four o'clock in the morning, we finished mixing the tracks, and I'd stagger home, knowing that the next day's work began at nine.

We taped the show on Thursday and Friday. In addition to the taping on those days, I was often called to production meetings. On Saturday and Sunday, I reintroduced myself to my family. On Monday the whole thing began again.

The incredible deadlines of television do little to foster creative expression. It's more important to write fast than to write well. With the intense and unyielding pressure of constant deadlines, it is little wonder that heart attacks are considered an occupational hazard for the television arranger. Several years later when we learned that the show would be cancelled, few of us were sad. I personally vowed never again to work on a weekly musical variety show. Besides, during that time something much more exciting was developing in my life.

Since my first experience with the acid rock bands at the Fillmore, I had had a recurring thought: Popular music is such an incredibly powerful medium of communication and influence—why has it so often been used in negative ways? Why couldn't it be used instead to influence young people positively? Why couldn't that powerful force build rather than destroy?

The Christian pop music movement had begun to flourish in the late sixties, and was, by this time, having quite an impact on Protestant youth. Ralph Carmichael, a leader of that movement, formed a company called Light Records and hired me to write music for one album based on the life of Paul, called "The Apostle," and another album based on the best-selling book by Hal Lindsey called *The Late Great Planet Earth*.

While there was much good in the Christian pop movement, I had several reservations about it. As its records became more profitable, it attracted many people whose only commitment was to making a fast buck. Moreover, I was offended by the frequent yoking of sacred words with irreverent music.

Even so, I felt that this same power could be used to reach our own Latter-day Saint youth. As a seminary teacher and Young Men's president, I observed many of our young people searching for contemporary heroes in an age of anti-heroes. If the music and entertainment of the world were so effective, I wondered why there were so few Latter-day Saint alternatives. I felt our youth reaching for something that they could not find. Sometimes they would settle for worldly substitutes.

Furthermore, I had met Latter-day Saints who came to Los Angeles eager to break into the entertainment industry without compromising their principles. I admired their desires, but in all honesty could give them little encouragement. I knew that as a Church we preached economic and physical self-sufficiency from the world, and I wondered why we couldn't become culturally self-sufficient as well. I longed for the day when Latter-day Saint music, television, and movie companies would produce our own artistically excellent alternatives to the world.

I knew it was time to act on my dream when author Carol Lynn Pearson showed me a manuscript of her play *The Order Is Love.* Lorin F. Wheelwright, dean of the College of Fine Arts at BYU, had committed to produce the show for the school's annual Mormon Festival of Arts in the spring of 1970. I agreed to write the music for the play. In partnership with Gerald Pearson, Carol Lynn's husband, I formed Embryo Music (so named because I envisioned great things from this small beginning) to publish the music and distribute the sound track from the play. The musical was produced to very enthusiastic audiences at BYU and is still being performed throughout the Church.

With Embryo formed, I needed something else to produce. But what? I observed that the Christian rock producers had discarded the cumbersome props and plot lines of traditional stage musicals to create a more direct proselyting tool. Their musicals usually consisted of a cycle of songs tied together with a few lines of dialogue. In reality, they were not musicals at all but what might be called pop rock oratorios.

This was the format I wanted to try for the Latter-day Saint audience. About this time, I became acquainted with Doug Stewart, who had recently moved into our ward. Although I knew nothing of his writing ability except that he had written one play at BYU (*A Day, a Night, and a Day*), I was impressed with his spirituality. We went with our wives to see one of these Protestant pop oratorios, "A Natural High" by Ralph Carmichael, at the First Baptist Church of Van Nuys.

The show was interesting, although anything but subtle. The producers had built a stage behind the pulpit of the huge chapel for performers and readers, while a rock band played in front of the pulpit. Although we found much of the show irreverent, we were amazed at its impact. Afterward, great numbers of people came forward to "accept" Jesus.

Adapting this musical form to an LDS audience presented at least three major problems. First, such a show could never take place in an LDS chapel. It would have to be performed in a theater. Second, the combining of sacred texts with irreverent music would be offensive to an LDS audience. Lyrics would have to focus on human relationships rather than on Deity. Any direct reference to scripture or Deity would be accompanied by an appropriately reverent musical style. Third, we had to communicate in the musical language of the youth without offending parents or Church leaders. We speculated that this could be accomplished by using a large choir to mask the contemporary rhythm and add a spiritual texture to the score; heavier rock music would be used only to portray evil. The result would be a middle-of-the-road pop sound.

With these parameters in mind, Doug and I went to work on a story. We threw around a number of plot ideas, but nothing clicked. We did create one vague character—a teenage boy in the midst of crisis. He doesn't get along with his family or with the Church. He is tempted by the world, and he doesn't really know what he wants from life. From that character we came up with a pivotal song called "Brace Me Up," which would ask the universal questions, "Who am I? Where am I going?" This was a beginning.

In January 1972, Doug was offered a job with the BYU Motion Picture Studios, and he moved back to Orem, Utah. We still had no real plot line and no new characters, although he sent me the lyrics for a song which would become "Voices"—still based on this character being pulled in different directions by his family and the world. When I met with Doug in June, he showed me a rough outline and a new song he had written for the title—*Saturday's Warrior*. We both knew it was right.

Working together on my visits to Utah, Doug's visits to LA, and through frequent letters, we developed the play through the summer and fall of 1972 and the winter of 1973. In April of 1973 we submitted it to the Utah State Playwriting Contest, and it was selected as one of the winners.

As a result, BYU agreed to produce it for the Mormon Festival of Arts in the spring of 1974. Doug and I continued to polish the show throughout the rest of 1973, readying it for its premiere the following spring. Although *Saturday's Warrior* was to become a turning point in my career, I was so busy at the time grinding out weekly shows for Sonny and Cher that I didn't give a full, concentrated effort to the music. I've since wondered if paying more attention to the score would have made it better ... or worse.

The opening of *Saturday's Warrior* was an important date

in my life. The show was an experiment to see if my dream of communicating gospel principles through the medium of contemporary music could be realized. Having watched the growing influence of music on huge masses of young people, I was anxious to see if this new musical form—something between a Christian pop rock oratorio and a traditional musical comedy—could be successful. With great anticipation, I attended the premiere performance of *Saturday's Warrior* at BYU on March 20, 1974.

That evening turned out to be one of the greatest disappointments of my life. Where I had envisioned a well-rehearsed choir seated in tuxedoes and formal gowns, I saw a few singer/dancers wandering around the stage in jeans and bare feet, attempting to blend the difficult choral harmonies between dance steps. The music, which was to be the central focus of this new art form, had been relegated to a secondary role.

To the extent that an orchestra or choir is choreographed, the music suffers, and the music and I suffered together. Too busy in LA to be present for any preproduction or rehearsals, I had failed to communicate my vision to the directors. About forty minutes into the performance, I couldn't take it anymore. My disappointment was so great that I became physically ill and had to leave the theater. Linda followed me and, after much persuasion, I returned to my seat. The fact that *Saturday's Warrior* received a standing ovation was little consolation (BYU audiences are known for their generosity). Needless to say, no one who saw my face that night asked what I thought of the production. For me, *Saturday's Warrior* had just died a horrible death and I never expected to see it produced again.

Professionally, this was a time of turmoil in my life. I still had moral reservations about my work in Hollywood, and had come to the conclusion that, at times, I was in the employ of Satan. Do Latter-day Saints belong in the entertainment business, I wondered, or are the compromises demanded too steep a price to pay? Were the monetary advantages of working in the music business distorting my view? On the other hand, if every morally committed person were to abandon his or her career in the entertainment business, wouldn't we be turning this important battlefront over to Satan without a fight? What was the right thing to do?

At the time Linda and I felt uneasy about living in Los Angeles because we had recently come through a meat shortage, a gasoline crisis, and a major earthquake (which caused the evacuation of our home), not to mention our continuing reservations about raising our children in a huge city. In the summer of 1974 we sold our home in Northridge, California, and bought a home in Lindon, Utah, although for the life of me I can't remember how I thought we would make a living there. I think we had some vague notions of commuting daily to Los Angeles or living off the land, growing strawberries in Pleasant Grove.

Just at this time, our California stake, the Chatsworth Stake, heard about the BYU production of *Saturday's Warrior* and asked if I would help produce the show as a fund-raising project. On one hand, I wanted to forget that the play even existed, but on the other, I was excited to see it produced as I had originally envisioned it. I agreed to help during the early stages of rehearsal, but told them that I would be in Utah during the actual performances.

When the show was cast and rehearsals were underway, my family prepared for our move to Utah. The night before we were scheduled to leave, the show had its first complete run-through with cast and choir. To that point, everyone had been rehearsing as if the production were just another roadshow, but that night we all realized that we were involved in something extraordinary. In the bare cultural hall of the Sherman Oaks Ward, we laughed, cried, and thrilled to the strains of the beautiful choir. I knew that evening that I would have to see the performances of the show. And so, not many weeks later, Linda, our four children and I returned from our new home in Lindon to set up camp in a spare bedroom in my mother's house and await the opening of the new production.

Chatsworth Stake had rented the Hall of Liberty at Forest Lawn Memorial Park for two performances of *Saturday's Warrior*. Both performances had sold out. In spite of a host of technical problems, the show somehow went on. I took my place in the audience along with 1800 other people, once again torn with opening-night anxiety. A man walked out and welcomed the audience. A missionary offered the prayer. The play began.

No one was prepared for what was to follow. Despite annoying feedback from the sound system, the audience howled at the funny lines, sobbed out loud in the tragic moments, and thrilled to the glorious crescendoes of the magnificent sixty-voice choir seated in front of the stage this time, wearing tuxedos and formal blue gowns. As I looked around at the audience, I sensed that something was happening that I had never experienced before—a magic, an electricity—call it what you will. All I know is that the show's impact exceeded my highest expectations. It really worked.

Within the next twenty-four hours, so many requests came in for more tickets that the Chatsworth Stake added two more nights to the scheduled performances. Doug and I were euphoric, but at the same time humbled at our success. We felt that all the experiences of our lives had been only a preparation for this one shining moment. We had somehow stumbled into a work which was much greater and more important than any of us.

At the cast party, Doug privately expressed his belief that we could keep the show alive by producing it on a private basis. At first I was offended at his suggestion. Although I had already published the music and released the soundtrack album for Embryo, somehow, in my mind, marketing records and music was different from making a profit from a spiritual experience. We discussed the idea for a while and decided to sleep on it. As the evening came to a close, everyone reluctantly said farewell, feeling that this once-in-a-lifetime experience was over.

The following day, Doug and his family returned to Orem, and we went back to Lindon. We found that we did not miss LA at all. Our children were making new friends, and it was a lovely time for us. Linda was relieved that we had settled down at last and could prepare for the birth of our fifth child.

Three days later the phone rang. It was Allen Blye, producer of *The Sonny and Cher Show* calling to say that the show had been cancelled. I felt releaved at being free from the weekly grind. Then he offered me the job of musical director on a new series, *The Sonny Bono Show*. I explained to him that I had moved to Utah "for good" and did not want to get involved in another weekly variety show.

In Hollywood, when you turn someone down, it means one thing—you want more money. The next day he called back to make another offer. I tried to explain the reasons for our move, the importance of a good environment for our children and the insecurity we had felt living in a large city. The following day he called back and raised the price considerably. At this point I became curious and asked why he wanted me. Compared to some of the big names, I was a nobody.

His response came as a great surprise. He said, "I want you

because I know you. I know where you're coming from, and I can trust you." I have reflected on his statement often since then. Apparently, values members of the Church tend to take for granted—integrity and loyalty—are so rare in some parts of the world that they are of great worth.

To make a long story short, two weeks later, we found ourselves back in LA, grinding out another weekly variety show, living without furniture in a rented house twenty feet from the Ventura Freeway.

Actually, there was an ulterior motivation for our move back to Los Angeles. In response to many requests to keep *Saturday's Warrior* alive, Doug and I had decided to reassemble the Los Angeles cast and produce the play on a free-enterprise basis. Could it really work? We weren't sure. As far as we knew, such a thing had never been done successfully before.

We rented the Pasadena High School auditorium to run twelve shows over four weeks in the fall of 1974. We bought the sets from the Chatsworth Stake, hired their Young Women's president, Ruth Latimer, to run the business end of it, and produced the show under the banner of Embryo Productions. Tickets were sold from the living room of our rented house. Day in and day out, Ruth and her staff would sit in that room, empty except for a batch of telephones and some borrowed chairs and lawn furniture, and answer the flood of calls for reservations.

The response was unbelievable. The phones never stopped ringing. For the first time in my experience, people lined up for hours to take investigator friends to a Church-oriented activity. We put chairs in the aisles of the theater. People bought tickets just to stand in the lobby with the hope of catching glimpses of the show. Reports began to filter in telling us of convert baptisms by the score and reconverted young lives.

At times, things got out of hand. People would bear their testimonies of *Saturday's Warrior*. At some meetings, words from the play were quoted alongside the scriptures. We had to remind people that the words "line upon line, precept upon precept" had first been written by Isaiah, not by Doug.

Eventually the four weeks passed. During that time, Rachel, our fifth child was born. Two days after the play closed, Doug returned to Utah, and I continued to work on *The Sonny Bono Show*, still convinced that we would move back to Lindon as soon as the television show ended (it was cancelled in November). Now that *Saturday's Warrior* was finished once and for all, we saw no further obstacle to moving back to Utah, where we felt we belonged.

Then the calls came in. People would not let the play die. Bishops, stake presidents, missionaries, and parents with troubled children, all called to ask when *Saturday's Warrior* would be produced again.

Finally, the full potential of this play hit Doug and me, and we decided to risk everything. We formed a company called Omega Productions. Doug borrowed thousands of dollars and I took out all my savings. We invested in sound and light systems, trucks, equipment, and stage rentals. Linda and I decided to stay in Los Angeles for just a few more months until we could get the company rolling.

We reopened the play with the LA cast in March of 1975. Later that cast toured many western states. In Phoenix they told us that we sold more tickets in two hours than Elton John sold in two weeks. Doug supervised a Utah production which opened in Spanish Fork and then moved to Salt Lake City for a grand total of one hundred twenty consecutive sold-out performances.

So we stayed on in our rented house in LA and I had plenty

of work in television. After *The Sonny Bono Show* was cancelled, I was hired as the musical director of *The Joey Heatherton Show*, and then of *Dick Van Dyke and Company*. I had various other freelance jobs during the mid-seventies, including the scoring of three films produced by a member of our ward, Lyman Dayton. They were *Where the Red Fern Grows, Against a Crooked Sky*, and *Baker's Hawk*.

Although these were my busiest years, one thought kept gnawing at my soul. Where should we raise our children? We had felt our decision to move to Utah was inspired, and yet we were still living in Los Angeles in a rented house next to a freeway, in the midst of all the things we wanted to escape. I had been struggling and praying about this problem for years, and I finally got a clear and definite but very personal answer in March of 1975. I was to be patient and try to grow spiritually where I was until the Lord made his will known to me in his own due time.

Within a couple of months, our landlord offered to let us buy the house we were living in for the same monthly payment as our rent. We decided to stay in Los Angeles, at least for the time being. Our move to Utah would have to wait. In "due time" we felt we did learn the will of the Lord when, in August of 1976, I was called to be bishop of the same ward I had grown up in. Since settling again in Los Angeles, we have come to feel that it does not matter where you live as much as how you live.

As it turned out, *Saturday's Warrior* became the turning point in my career because it enabled me to write music aimed more and more at the LDS community and less and less "at the world." Because of the success of *Saturday's Warrior*, our names came to the attention of Elder L. Tom Perry, chairman of the bicentennial committee of the Church. Doug and I were selected to write a bicentennial production for the Church.

I enjoyed some of the greatest spiritual experiences of my life while working on the music for this production. Although the play, *Threads of Glory*, never gained great popular acceptance, it resulted in spiritual growth for both Doug and me. Those familiar with Church history will know what I mean when I say that *Threads of Glory* became our personal "Zion's Camp."

Shortly after *Saturday's Warrior* had been produced, I approached Carol Lynn Pearson about writing a cycle of gospel songs for a children's album. We worked on those songs on and off throughout 1976, and decided to turn them into a children's musical. Carol Lynn wrote a script tying the songs together, and *My Turn On Earth* was produced successfully in both Utah and Los Angeles.

My Turn On Earth was important for several reasons. First, it showed us that *Saturday's Warrior* was not just an accident. Secondly, *My Turn On Earth* had no choir, no large cast, no complex story line. With its entire cast of five, it could play in much more intimate surroundings. Latter-day Saint audiences proved to be just as willing to support simple plays as big productions. Interestingly enough, both *Saturday's Warrior* and *My Turn On Earth* have qualified for gold albums, despite lack of air play and distribution through traditional record outlets.

Shortly after *My Turn On Earth* was produced, I heard Heather Young, a well-known actress in the Los Angeles area, give a fireside based on an imaginary diary of a young Mormon girl faced with all the various temptations of our modern age. Together, Heather and I turned this concept into a musical play. *Debbie: Diary of Mormon Girl* opened in San Gabriel, California, on September 18, 1978.

The success of these plays and other albums and projects came concurrently with my calling as bishop and gave me a

certain degree of economic independence from the Hollywood music community. This freedom has enabled me to turn
down studio work of questionalble moral content as well as
projects with time demands that would interfere with my
calling as bishop. It has been a great blessing to be able to
combine two things I love dearly—music and the gospel.

I am grateful to be living in a day when the LDS
community is large enough to support a culture of its own. As
I view the recent proliferation of LDS novels, music, and
drama, I realize we are standing on the verge of a great
explosion of LDS cultural achievement. Although some
criticize these fledgling attempts on the basis of "artistic
merit" or their "commercialization of Mormonism," I see
such endeavors as a healthy sign of a hopeful future. The
emergence of the Mormon market will encourage production
of an increasing number of moral cultural works. From this
increasing quantity will appear some works of enduring
artistic worth.

I am encouraged by the increased output of Mormon
entertainment and art for another reason. Entertainment can
be a powerful teaching tool. No one knows this better than the
master of the "soft sell," Satan himself. He knows that people
can be taught very effectively when they are unaware that they
are being taught—when they think they are only being
entertained.

For several decades now, observant Latter-day Saints have
watched Satan proselyte the unsuspecting masses through
motion pictures, television, radio and literature. We have sat
back watching, almost helplessly, unable and unprepared to
offer a viable alternative. If we are to do battle in the war for
the minds of men, we must learn to fight with the weapons of
our time. Powerful sermons need not be limited to the pulpit
alone. For example, no greater sermon could be preached on

genealogy than the one Alex Haley preached in *Roots*.

I have chosen music as my weapon to fight in the battle. I do not consider myself an "artist." I am more interested in music as a vehicle to communicate ideas than as an abstract art form. Although I have great respect for those who spend years building durable monuments of art, I have chosen to write in popular idioms because popular music is the language of the people. I do want to create great artistic music sometime, but I don't feel that time will come until the next life, when I may finally be able to sit down at my Steinway with eternity before me. As for this life, I would rather make my contribution as a missionary than as an artist.

The Power of Music

A terrible thing
is music in general...
Music makes me forget
my real situation.
It transports me into a state
which is not my own.
Under the influence of music
I really seem to feel
what I do not understand,
to have powers which
I cannot have.

Tolstoy,
The Kreutzer Sonata, *XXIII*

Chapter 1

Music
and the Body

*To study rhythm is to study all of music. Rhythm both
organizes and is itself organized by all the elements which
create and shape music processes.*

Mursell

*When the musics from all cultures of the world are
considered, it is rhythm that stands out as most
fundamental. Rhythm is the organizer and the energizer.
Without rhythm, there would be no music, whereas there
is much music that has neither melody nor harmony.*

Gaston

The issue of music's influence on bodily functions is not
completely a product of modern scientific research. Many
ancient peoples used music as a healing agent; in fact, in many
mythologies, the god of music is also the god of medicine.

In recent years, a vast number of studies have substanti-
ated these ancient beliefs, demonstrating music's effect on a
myriad of bodily functions and on performance of physical
activity, including: pulse rate, respiration rate, blood pressure,
galvanic skin response, brain wave impulses, muscle response,
finger coordination, reading speed and comprehension,
arithmetic skills, responses to medical operations, bicycle
skills, basketball techniques, and more.[1]

Music as a tool in the treatment of disturbed individuals
has been the subject of literally thousands of studies. In fact,
the National Association of Musical Therapy (NAMT) even
awards an RMT (Registered Musical Therapist) degree.
Between 1960 and 1976, over 2,000 articles were published in

422 different periodicals on the topic of musical therapy.[2]

Not surprisingly, some believe that the music and noise in our homes directly influence our mental and physical health. Dr. Steven Halpern, lecturing at the University of North Carolina's Asheville campus, recently stated that every molecule in our body gives off and receives vibrations with a certain frequency. He claims that our internal organs combine to give us constant "biosymphony" within our bodies.

When we find music that is in tune with our bodies, we feel less stress and more serenity. The sounds of nature as well as the flute, harp, electric piano, bells, and such meditative and invigorating works as Bach's *B Minor Mass* all harmonize with the natural vibrations of our bodies.

The constant whir of a refrigerator, on the other hand, can gradually wear on our inner calm until we become stressed, cranky, hungry, and unhealthy, even though we are not conscious of that background noise. Loud, dissonant, or vigorous music (even Beethoven's) does not encourage meditation or inner calm. Dr. Halpern claims that we must maintain our resistance to harsh, harmful noise by filling our minds regularly with strengthening music.[3]

How does music wield this tremendous influence? The answer seems to lie in the power of rhythm.

More than any other element of music—more than melody, harmony, dynamics, or instrumentation—it is rhythm which elicits a powerful physical response from man. It is rhythm that determines whether our toes will tap, our fingers snap, our hands clap, our feet march, our bodies sway and jerk, or our minds relax into deep contemplation. Whatever our response to a particular piece of music, rhythm is usually the instigator.

I love rhythm! It is much of the fun and excitement of music. It is energy and power. A general uses martial strains to prepare his country for war, the bishop uses the martial "Onward Christian Soldiers" to encourage his ward to work at the welfare farm—an invigorating rhythm gets us up and going. It works!

Although all music has rhythm, not all music has a strongly marked pulse. Some music has no pulse at all. Music with a weak pulse tends to elicit a passive response from the listener and is often helpful in encouraging meditative and contemplative moods, reverence, or even sleep. It can tranquilize. Lullabies, hymns, chorales, and legato string music tend to produce this effect.

At the other end of the spectrum, vigorous music with a strongly marked pulse such as marches, dances, and even Beethoven's fiery works, is not music to meditate by. Throughout the ages, composers of all styles of music have recognized and exploited the physical and emotional power of rhythm. It is rhythm which gives energy and vitality to the "Hallelujah Chorus" of Handel's *Messiah*. Interestingly enough, the straight eighth note rhythm of the "Hallelujah Chorus" also forms the foundation of much of today's rock music. Composers of both sacred and popular music can use a strong pulse to excite an audience.

At one extreme of the rhythmic spectrum lies music with such an intense pulse (strengthened by electronic amplification) that it discourages intellectual activity and sweeps aside normal mental inhibitions in favor of a purely physical response. Rock music is controversial largely because some see this overwhelming physical response as animalistic.

Recent studies have even suggested that certain marked beats may actually weaken our muscles. For several years I worked out regularly at a health club to the heavy beat of an FM rock station. At times, I sensed that I was becoming weak and tired long before I should have. I felt so much stress from trying to work out to the music that I finally quit the club and joined another one where they played no music at all.

I recently read a book by Dr. John Diamond which may explain what I was experiencing. Dr. Diamond discovered that certain kinds of music could actually weaken the muscles of his test subjects. He contends that while the average deltoid muscle (the one that hold up your arm) can normally withstand forty to forty-five pounds of pressure, it can withstand only about fifteen pounds while certain rock music is played. He theorizes that this is the result of the rock rhythm.

Much rock music uses an anapestic beat (ba-ba-bop, ba-ba-bop) which has a jerking, frustrated energy. The waltz, on the other hand, has just the opposite beat (bop-ba-ba, bop-ba-ba) and does not have this weakening effect on the muscles. Dr. Diamond explains that this anapestic beat somehow acts as an inhibiting influence on the thymus gland, which is responsible for directing the internal flow of energy to the muscles.

Having tested over twenty thousand records on different subjects, he found that most music does not have this weakening effect. Most classics, jazz, country and western, and even music by the Beatles and early rock 'n roll (preceding the harder rock of the mid-sixties) do not weaken the muscles. But much of the music of Led Zeppelin, The Doors, The Band, Janis Joplin, Alice Cooper, and even America, among many others, does.[4]

A force so powerful that it can influence our hearts, our glands, and our muscles is a force to be reckoned with. Throughout history, music has been used in religious ceremonies, on the battlefield, in hospitals and schoolrooms, in industry, advertising, and politics as a potent persuasive tool. From the ten-month old baby who bounces to a beat even though he or she can neither walk nor talk, to the aged person who seeks solace in edifying and contemplative music, we are all subject to its power. Music has found so many uses and purposes because of one simple fact. It can influence people's lives.

Chapter 2

Music and Emotions

Explain it as we may, a martial strain will urge a man into the front rank of battle sooner than an argument, and a fine anthem excite his devotion more certainly than a logical discourse.

Tuckerman

Music has been called the universal language. It is a language more powerful than words, for it is the language of emotion. Words communicate ideas; music communicates feelings. While words get stuck in the thinking part of our brains, music sails through to reach the innermost corners of our emotional being. And it is our emotions and feelings which really govern our lives and our actions. This is precisely why music is such a wonderful, dangerous, exhilarating, exciting power.

An example: While writing music for the film *Where the Red Fern Grows*, I encountered a problem. The entire story was built around a boy's love for his two dogs, and the audience needed to feel that love in order for the film to work. But on the bare celluloid, that important emotion was missing. I composed a tender love theme to fill that void. From the first time the dogs appeared as cute, cuddly little puppies to the end of the show when they died, the theme or one of its variations was played every time they appeared on the screen. Suddenly the flat images on strips of celluloid had emotional life! The audience wept.

Film scoring exists in large part to manipulate our emotions. Listen for "Tara's Theme" the next time you see *Gone*

With the Wind. It is played over and over and over to involve us emotionally in the story. Music in film can build the suspense, fear, romance, loneliness, sensuality, comedy, celebration, or joy in any scene. It can, in fact, change the intent of an entire scene. If overdone or done melodramatically, music can turn a tense chase scene into high comedy, a love scene into a farce. Try adding some background music the next time you watch home movies. They will come to life for you.

Music's emotional superiority over words can perhaps be seen best in stage musicals. Words can take a scene only so far. Once the "I love you's" have been said—even if they have been said with much passion—it is left to the music to carry the emotion to unspoken heights. Musical plays draw larger audiences than non-musical plays because they cause us to feel things more deeply.

Perhaps music communicates emotions so effectively because, more than any other single art form, it possesses the properties of human emotions. For instance, a person may feel elated or depressed for long periods or may experience either emotion with the speed of thought. His emotions have velocity. They may build to a peak. They have intensity. A person may feel several emotions simultaneously—experiencing jealousy and joy, or anger and love at the same time.

Music is able to duplicate these many emotional elements. Music has elation and depression (high and low notes), velocity (allegro and adagio), intensity (crescendo and diminuendo), and simultaneous emotions (contrasting textures). Music has been called "the royal art medium of emotion."[5]

When asked to explain jazz, Louis Armstrong said, "If you have to explain it, forget it." Either you feel it or you don't. Music is as near to pure emotion as any art form can come. It makes us feel deeply, and therein lies its great power.

Chapter 3

Music
and Memory

"Darling, they're playing our song."
Anonymous

Some time ago my wife and I were driving together when
she turned on the radio. On came "Summer in the City" by
the Lovin' Spoonful. We had not heard that song in over a
decade. Yet before a single note was sung—in just the first
two bars of the introduction—we were instantly transported
back to July of 1966, the year we were married and travelled to
San Francisco on our honeymoon.

Suddenly we were sitting in that rented red Mustang,
driving across the Golden Gate Bridge. We could smell the
musky interior of the vinyl seats. Linda looked lovely that day.
She was just nineteen. Her dark Arizona tan shone out against
her bone-colored dress. She was blonder then and wore her
hair in a flip. We headed down into Sausalito and pulled into
the Trident Restaurant, where we spent several hours over a
leisurely lunch, watching the sailboats in the bay. Although we
hadn't heard that song in years, we were able to relive that
delightful experience because of two bars of a song.

Consider a negative example of the same principle. A
mother is driving her little daughter to school. A light, happy
tune is playing on the radio. Suddenly they see an oncoming
car in their lane. There is a terrible crash and the child is killed.
Will the mother ever hear that song again without reliving
the whole tragic experience? The same tune may seem light
and happy to others, but for her it will evoke only feelings of

terror and sadness.

Music seems to go into the long-term memory of our brains. The replaying of a few notes of a song may instantly bring back not only the song itself, but a whole flood of other memories associated with it, be those recollections memories of good or bad parts of our lives.

This principle is vital to any discussion of morality and music. A song which may be harmless in itself can take on the moral overtones of the experiences or environment associated with it. The "electric gee-tar" had drug associations for the man mentioned in the introduction. Similarly, the sitar, a respectable instrument of ancient India, became associated almost exclusively with the American drug culture of the sixties. It is difficult for some to hear the sitar played without remembering those early days of drug exploration.

Worshippers in Solomon's temple used instruments such as the ram's horn, and others similar to the modern-day harp, flute, trumpet, cymbal, drum, bell, and tambourine. To the ancient Israelites, these instruments were associated with feelings of praise, joy, and thanksgiving. When the temple was destroyed shortly after Lehi left Jerusalem, instruments were eliminated from the worship service as a symbol of mourning over the destruction of the temple. Because these instruments had taken on such a sacred quality by their association with the temple, they were not used again until the temple was rebuilt about half a century later.

Although there is no scriptural reason to avoid using music in temple worship today, drums, cymbals, tambourines, and trumpets have such worldly associations in the minds of most Latter-day Saints that we might feel uncomfortable if such instruments were used even in Sunday worship services, let alone in the temple. The instruments that once carried holy associations to ancient Israel carry no such holy associations to most people today. Thus, there are times when music becomes appropriate or inappropriate because of its associations rather than because of the innate qualities of the music itself.

Because of its impact upon memory, music is an effective tool in learning and retaining information. The earliest Gregorian chants helped the monks memorize a prescribed liturgy. How many seminary students have been able to memorize the books of the Old Testament by learning them in song form? We all know how effectively Primary songs and hymns teach gospel principles.

Music can be an instant recall mechanism. We can relive spiritually uplifting moments as well as times we should forget. Images, good and evil, parade before our minds when we hear the music associated with them. Music is an effective means of indoctrination. We do not soon forget that which we learn with music.

Chapter 4

The Power of Music and Words

W hen words are set to music, they gain new powers. Consider the following "poem" from the early 1960's:

You think you lost your love
Well I saw her yesterday
It's you she's thinking of
And she told me what to say
She says she loves you
And you know that can't be bad
Yes, she loves you
And you know you should be glad
Whooooo.
She loves you
Yeah, yeah, yeah.
She loves you
Yeah, yeah, yeah.[6]

This is hardly Pulitzer Prize-winning material. And yet, when these words were set to a free-swinging, infectious tune, they created an irresistible force. Millions of teenagers literally climbed over each other to purchase more than three million singles of this record.

How many copies of this poem would have sold had it not been set to music? It's doubtful that teenagers could stand the boredom of reciting the words even once without the music, yet how many millions of times have those same empty lyrics been listened to and repeated merely because they were accompanied by music? The music supplies the power and the energy, and words add concrete images to music's abstract emotional power.

Occasionally, the situation is reversed and clever lyrics give life to rather bland melodies. In the late sixties, Paul Simon, Jim Morrison, and Bob Dylan created highly influential lyrics which became more important than the melodies themselves. But this was the exception rather than the rule. Usually, the music gives a song its emotional power, while lyrics tie that power to a concrete idea. Generally, lyrics appeal to the head while music captures the heart.

The lyrics of "She Loves You" were rather innocuous, but the situation becomes serious when questionable or immoral words are wedded to an appealing melody. This was never clearer to me than when I was hired to make an instrumental version of the song "Do That To Me One More Time" by Captain and Tennille. I didn't care much for the tune and cared even less for the erotic words. In order to take the melody and harmony off the record, however, I had to play it at least a dozen times. Even though I was making an instrumental version and wasn't interested in the words at all, I could not get the melody or the words out of my mind for days afterward. Hard-to-remember words stick in the mind easily when combined with catchy, easy-to-remember melodies. That song kept returning to haunt me. Ironically, I didn't even like the song. What if I *had* liked it?

Music is the sugar coating on the pill that helps the "bitter" lyrics go down. We may become so infatuated with the rhythm, melody, singer, or "feel" of a song that we transfer this adoring emotion to the words, not caring what they really say. Even if they are erotic, drug-oriented, violent, satanic, or just plain silly, when tied to a "hit" tune, they sneak past the screening mechanism of the brain to be stored in our subconscious forever. Think of how many times some of those "hit" songs are listened to. We may say, "I don't listen to the lyrics," but so-called "unlistened-to" lyrics can be far more influential than the same words spoken.

Some Moral Considerations

Music makes anything go.
It makes a peace meeting more peaceful,
it intensifies the spirit of courage
in soldiers, it makes drunkards drink more,
it seduces, it uplifts,
it stimulates workers, it soothes and it heals.
We are to decide its use,
destructive or constructive.

Harriet A. Seymour

Chapter 1

Relative Versus Eternal Standards

Parents have always been concerned about the moral effects of the younger generation's music. In Meredith Wilson's *The Music Man*, set in the early 1900's, Professor Harold Hill attempts to convince the parents that they need a youth orchestra to help their children avoid the perils of the local pool hall. In the monologue "Ya Got Trouble," he calls ragtime that "shameless music, grabs your son and your daughter with the arms of a jungle animal instanct, masteria!"[1]

This is a humorous treatment of a moral question with which many have wrestled. How many parents today would be grateful to have their children listening to ragtime instead of hard rock? Indeed, today we see that "shameless music" as nothing more than a historical relic with little moral significance to our society.

A letter from the First Presidency requested members to refrain from "dances that require or permit the close embrace and suggestive movements" and pleaded that we "let not the brilliant prospects of a glorious millenium be clouded with such shadows as are threatened by customs and costumes and diversions of these licentious days."[2] When were "these licentious days"? The letter was written in 1912. What "suggestive" dance was condemned? The waltz.

Even in Sister Camilla Kimball's recent biography, she

tells us that the first time a man tried to waltz with her, she feared she was being "morally assaulted."[3] How is it that a child caught dancing the waltz in 1912 might have been punished, while a child found dancing the waltz today might be given a raise in allowance? Has the gospel changed? Is it not eternally the same?

The answer is both yes and no. The eternal principles of purity of thought and modesty will never change, but the application of those principles may change from society to society or from time to time. It is important to understand the meaning a particular dance style carries for a particular society.

The common dances before the waltz came into fashion were the "reel," "line," and "square" dances where partners changed several times during each dance and men did not hold women in a direct way. With the waltz, a man held the same woman throughout the dance in a much more intimate way than ever before. Thus, a couple raised on Virginia reels, who suddenly embraced each other one-on-one in a waltz, could very well have had a sensual experience.

Today it is not the waltz, but other dances which have that effect on many people. Those are the dances which concern us as parents and youth leaders today. Thus, the principles are eternal, but the practices and interpretations of those eternal principles may be somewhat changeable and relative.

History offers many examples of changing style. A man or a woman who went swimming a hundred years ago dressed in one of today's "modest" bathing suits would have created a scandal. At one time a clean-shaven face and slicked-down hair were considered to be a sign of following the extreme fashions of the world, whereas today they are standard attire for all missionaries and most Church leaders. Ragtime was once the symbol of extreme worldliness in music, but now it is considered almost quaint. The real issue is often not the hair or the bathing suit or a particular musical category, but the meaning of those things to a society. Such items are often seen as outward signs of an inward attitude.

Although in the past one hundred fifty years it has been possible for Latter-day Saints to follow somewhat in the wake of the world's fashions, it would be a serious mistake to assume that we may always do so. There are some limits which may not be passed, some worldly trends which will never be acceptable no matter how firmly entrenched they become in society. As the culture of the modern world approaches that of Sodom and Gomorrah, Latter-day Saints are seeing an increasing need to draw the line.

Some music is acceptable in one setting but not in another. Although Dixieland music is highly appropriate for the park, it would be offensive to any spiritually sensitive person in a sacrament meeting. The loud, brassy, upbeat style is inherently incompatible with the reverent, contemplative mood of a sacrament meeting. Furthermore, in our society, Dixieland music evokes worldly associations that would tend to draw our thoughts away from the spiritual purpose of a sacrament service.

Then what sort of music is appropriate for worship services? This is not a simple case of pop versus classical music. The purpose of music in church is to help the congregation focus on spiritual thoughts and glorify God. So any music which focuses itself on the world, the composer, or the performer, is inappropriate. Both classical and pop music may fall into this category. On the other hand, both styles can be used to lift us spiritually. "I Am a Child of God," most Primary songs, and many hymns are basically "popular" in style because of their simple, memorable, and regular melodies, harmonies, and rhythms.

Some feel that because classical music is on a higher intellectual level, it is also on a higher spiritual level. Nothing could be further from the truth. Intellectuality is not synonymous with spirituality. When I hear musicians perform such works as Beethoven's "Sonata Pathetique" or De Falla's "Ritual Dance of Fire" in church, I wonder if the work is performed to glorify God or as a virtuostic display to glorify the performer.

Chapter 2

"Good" Art Versus Moral Art

S ome time ago, I heard a new song on the radio. It was very well done. The creator had skillfully combined some unusual electronic sounds, and I was impressed. I wanted to hear the song again and even considered buying the record (something I rarely do). Later that day, the song was played again. This time I listened to the words. The song was completely immoral. It was one of the best immoral songs I had ever heard!

Today we are continually confronted with "good" art and entertainment that are immoral in intent. According to the thirteenth Article of Faith, "If there is anything virtuous, lovely, or of good report, or praiseworthy, we seek after these things." Some have interpreted this to mean, "If there is anything of good report *according to art critics,* or praiseworthy *according to the world,* we seek after these things, *regardless of their moral implications.* Unfortunately, there are Latter-day Saints who indulge in immoral entertainment and art and justify their actions on the grounds that those works have artistic merit.

I am not recommending that Latter-day Saints settle for mediocrity in the arts or in any other aspect of their lives. I lament the lack of good moral art from which to choose in today's world. I am also saddened by the fact that Satan appears to be more effective than we are in using the power of the arts to proselyte. This is not meant as a criticism of Latter-day Saints, but as a challenge for us to reach up and excel in the production of high quality works of art and entertainment *with moral intent.*

Nevertheless, there is no excuse for us to embrace anything which is immoral in purpose. Satan must be smiling with the knowledge that he has only to bait his hooks with words like *art, masterpiece, award winning,* and *top ten* to reel in thousands of victims eager to pay for their own indoctrination. Simply stated, immorality has no place in the life of a Latter-day Saint, no matter how popular it is or how well it is done.

All this leads us to the crucial question—how do we judge the morality of a work? We judge it by the most revealing criterion of all—by its intent.

Chapter 3

Judging the Work: Its Intent

In pop music today, many songs communicate a message, and that message may be moral, neutral, or immoral. Usually the message is communicated by words, but not always. In the song "Love to Love You Baby," Donna Summer's moans and groans may not be words found in the dictionary, but her message is clear. It is difficult for purely instrumental music to communicate specific ideas without the help of a title or program, but it can communicate emotions or feelings such as joy, tranquility, humor, anxiety, anger, chaos, and frustration.

To judge the morality of a song, or any other work of art, we must look at its intent. An immoral intent will usually reveal itself in one of three ways:

1. The work may blatantly preach a message;
2. The work may attempt to cause an audience to empathize with a certain message; or
3. The work may present an unbalanced or disproportionate view of good and evil.

Preachment

A few years ago, Billy Joel released the hit song "Only the Good Die Young" in which he preaches to religious girls to give up their virginity:

Come out Virginia
Don't let me wait
You Catholic girls
Start much too late
But sooner or later
It comes down to fate
I might as well be the one...
They say there's a heaven
For those who will wait
Some say it's better
But I say it ain't
I'd rather laugh with the sinners
Than cry with the saints
Sinners are much more fun
And only the good die young.[4]

The words and message of this song are obvious. It is an example of a song which blatantly preaches—it is a sermon for immorality.

Such songs are increasing with alarming rapidity. Not too long ago, songs had to disguise their immoral messages. As Peter, Paul and Mary sang their hit of the mid-sixties:

I dig rock 'n' roll music...
But if we really say it
The radio won't play it
Unless we lay it between the lines.[5]

Anyone who listens to today's pop music will know that this is definitely no longer the case.

Empathy

A more dramatic way to legitimize immorality is to tell a story which glorifies it and creates empathetic feelings in the listener. Several years ago a song called "Oh, What a Night," told the story of a young man's first sexual experience:

You know I didn't even know her name
But I was never going to be the same
What a lady, what a night.[6]

The song glorifies and describes the couple's immorality. It tries to make the audience understand the boy's enthusiasm and thus empathize with him. And it attempts to create the same desires in its listeners.

Empathy can be a more effective method of persuasion than preaching. A preachment is an appeal to the intellect, whereas empathy is an appeal to the emotions. A certain message may be analyzed and rejected by the intellect but accepted by the less discerning emotions. Music, the art medium of the emotions, is the ideal vehicle to appeal to the empathetic side of our natures.

Balance

Although some songs may neither preach nor seem to empathize with wrong-doing, they portray evil so much more graphically than good that they focus our minds on evil as much as if it were being preached outright. The second biggest-selling album in America in 1981 was *Paradise Theatre* by Styx. One of its songs is called "Snowblind." (*Snow* is a street word for cocaine.) It seems as if the singer is lamenting his addiction:

Harmless and innocent you devil in white
You stole my will without a fight
You filled me with confidence
But you blinded my eyes
You tricked me with visions of Paradise
Now I realize that I'm snowblind
Can't live without you.

At first, this might seem to be an anti-drug song. But near the end the singer exclaims:

> *Mirror, mirror, I confess*
> *I can't escape this emptiness*
> *No more reasons to pretend*
> *Here comes that same old feeling again*
> *I'm snowblind, can't live without you*
> *Cause you're so fine, can't get away.*[7]

Then he gives in to another cocaine trip which is accompanied by high, euphoric voices and guitar riffs. It is possible to talk about cocaine, perhaps even to sing about it, without promoting it but in this song the joys of cocaine are emphasized more than its horrors. Although the singer laments that he is hooked, he fascinates the listener into wondering what is "so fine" about this drug.

A more recent and more complex example is the 1982 hit, "I've Never Been to Me." In this song, an immoral young woman regrets her immorality and says that while she's been all over the world and experienced all types of "thrills," she's "never been to me." That is, she's never discovered her true inner spiritual identity. The fact that she realizes her mistake is praiseworthy. Unfortunately, in recounting her past errors, she describes her sexual immorality in such alluring language that one begins to wonder if the purpose of the song isn't really to glorify her lifestyle rather than to warn against it.

Although there are shades of gray with these kinds of lyrics, we should not forget that when evil is presented so graphically and dwelt upon excessively, it has the effect of fixing the listener's mind upon that evil and breaking down barriers that would normally be present. Alexander Pope wrote:

Vice is a monster of so frightful mien,
As, to be hated, needs but to be seen;
Yet seen too oft, familiar with her face,
We first endure, then pity, then embrace.[8]

Much of today's music dwells so excessively on evil that it aids in that "pitying, then embracing" process.

The issue of how to appropriately speak about evil has always been a touchy one. In attempting to describe the disastrous effects of sin, it is easy to get so graphic that the listener's curiosity is aroused and his mind fixed on the very evil which should be avoided. It is almost as tempting to go to the other, equally harmful, extreme and present a white-washed, simplistic picture of life wherein evil is so trivialized as to be nonthreatening and almost nonexistent.

Over a century ago, an English theologian and musical philosopher, H.A. Haweis, commented on this problem: "Nothing can be falser than to suppose that morality is served by representing facts other than they are; no emasculated picture of life can be moral—it may be meaningless, and it is sure to be false."[9] In creating art or entertainment we must neither mask the true dangers of life nor dwell upon evil in an explicit or disproportionate way. Finding the delicate balance between the two extremes is often difficult, but it is always important.

Haweis summarizes the basic issue succinctly:

Does the artist show that his sympathies lie with an unwholesome preponderance of horrible, degraded, or of simply pleasurable, as distinct from healthy, emotions? Is he for whipping the jaded senses to their work, or merely for rejoicing in the highest activity of their healthful exercise? Does he love what is good whilst acknowledging the existence of evil, or does he delight in what is evil and

merely introduce what is good for the vicious sake of
trampling upon it?... The highest service that art can
accomplish for man is to become at once the voice of his
nobler aspirations, and the steady disciplinarian of his
emotions.[10]

Songs need not be judged solely on their lyrics. Album
covers, which are often pornographic, satanic, or drug-related,
also provide a clue to a group's intent. Many groups also make
videotaped versions of their songs for play on cable television
and other media which might promote album sales. These
tapes are not mere recordings of the group in concert, but an
intricate and sophisticated interweaving of concert performances, animation, and drama. Rapid-editing techniques give
a flashy, attention-grabbing, often science fiction, surrealistic,
or even erotic "feel" to the performance.

When we hear R.E.O. Speedwagon sing "When I said that
I love you I meant/That I love you forever,"[11] we may be
tempted to think that they are singing about eternal marriage.
But their videotaped version of the song, which is frequently
intercut with scenes of a prostitute hanging on all the
members of the band, proves that their interpretation of
eternal love and ours have nothing in common. And if Rod
Stewart's lyrics were not blatant enough, who can doubt his
true intent while watching him openly grab his genitals in a
live concert recently broadcast over the public airwaves?

Unfortunately, we must still listen to the lyrics of some
groups to determine if their songs preach evil, persuade us to
emphathize with evil, or show evil in an unbalanced light. But
much of the heated debate about the subtle meaning of certain
songs can now be put to rest as groups manifest their true
intent with increasing openness.

Chapter 4

Morality
and the Artist

"Why don't you kids learn to appreciate real music—classical music—instead of idolizing those immoral rock stars?"

"You think rock stars are immoral? Did you ever read about Wagner and Liszt?"

These questions raised at the fireside mentioned in the introduction to this book strike at the heart of some very important issues. First, are artists and entertainers less moral as a class than other segments of society? Second, why are we so willing to overlook the immorality of great artists of the past and so quick to condemn the immorality of present-day rock stars?

Although the history of music must admit to its Liszts, Paganinis, and Wagners with their scandalous escapades, it can also hold up its Haydns, Bachs, Mozarts, and Mendelssohns who lived virtuous lives by any standard. I don't think we can generalize that artists of the past and present have lived less moral lives as a group than any other members of their society. If the lives of private citizens were as open to public scrutiny as the lives of our celebrities, we might discover the same vices in a similar proportion.

Nevertheless, there is a problem which is unique to the arts and the entertainment industry. Many professions have built-in restraints against open immorality. A dishonest accountant might cheat us. A pharmacist who is a drunk or a drug addict might poison us. Few people would go to a doctor if they knew he were involved in Satan worship or witchcraft. A lawyer given to open violence might destroy our chances in court. A police officer or a member of congress who is a sexual deviate might be subject to blackmail. Yet all these vices are openly admitted by some celebrities today. So long as he or she performs well, an adoring public readily overlooks all his or her immoralities.

Indeed, the easiest way to break through the fierce competition in the entertainment industry and get the public's attention is through notorious and outrageous behavior. Sensationalism is often the ticket to success. Society actually seems to applaud and encourage immorality on the part of its celebrities. It is as if the public vicariously lives out its own immoral fantasies through the lives of its superstars. The real cause may lie in the public's hidden desire for sin as much as in the celebrities' immoral inclinations. The first encourages, rewards, and appears to demand the latter.

The question has long been debated: Do art and entertainment reflect the moral climate of society or create it? The answer is, they do both. The audience must bear much of the responsibility for the moral quality of art and artists. Whenever we support a work of art of any moral color, we vote for more of the same.

Let's look more closely at the second question raised: Why are we so willing to overlook the immorality of the great artists of the past and so quick to condemn the immorality of present-day rock stars? Perhaps the following example can clarify this issue. It is said that Peter Illyich Tchaikovsky struggled with the problem of homosexuality. A popular group today called The Village People openly advocates homosexuality. Is there a difference buying a Tchaikovsky recording and a Village People recording? Yes, there is a big difference. Today the art of media manipulation and public relations is a highly refined skill. It is the image of a group (including their name, album covers, stage reputation, and publicized attitudes) which sells albums as much as the music itself. The image of The Village People is carefully groomed to promote homosexuality. All of their music, live performances, and costumes are built around this theme. The humor in their hits "Macho Man," "YMCA," and "In the Navy" can only be understood in a homosexual context. They sell more than music, and when we buy their albums we buy more than music. They use music to popularize, exploit, and promote homosexuality. They are missionaries for the movement.

On the other hand, Tchaikovsky's life was dedicated to the composition of great music, not to the promotion of homosexuality through music. He wrestled with his personal problem on a private level. His music may have reflected the intensity of his emotional struggles, but it cannot be said that he used his art to proselyte for homosexuality. Tchaikovsky wrote great music *in spite* of this weakness, but The Village People have become popular *because* of it. The essence of the issue is this: the music of The Village People promotes homosexuality; the music of Peter Illyich Tchaikovsky does not.

In pop music today, there are those committed to equally offensive causes—Satanism (Black Sabbath), violence (the Plasmatics), and drug abuse (China White). Others use music to proselyte for various religions such as Baha'i (Seals and Crofts), Hare Krishna (George Harrison, at one time), and various forms of "born again" Christianity (Andre Crouch and Debbie Boone). Although "born again" Christian rock may be more palatable than satanic music, at times it may be equally offensive to a Latter-day Saint. The question is, where do we draw the line?

When a performer's life is committed to a specific cause, we know, at least, where he stands, and we can make a blanket acceptance or rejection of his work if we choose to. But today, in the arts as in all segments of society, many have only one cause—to make money. Performers in this category (the majority) may perform several moral or neutral songs and then include some outrageously immoral songs to help sell the album. In other words, they will record whatever sells.

What do we do now? Should we reject an album with nine innocent songs and one immoral one? Should we reject everything an artist has done or will do because of one song or one movie which was immoral? Can the same song be moral or neutral if performed by one artist but immoral when recorded by another to whom we object? Is an instrumental version of an immoral song equally immoral?

These are the gray areas where choices can be difficult. It is in this gray area, however, where most of life's decisions are made. Each individual and each family must draw their own lines as to how much evil they will tolerate. Each individual decision is important, and the effects of our choices become more apparent when viewed from an eternal perspective.

Our challenge is to become celestial people while living in a telestial world. In order to accomplish this we must come out of the world, forsake the world, and not be "of the world." This telestial world produces primarily telestial art and entertainment. To immerse ourselves indiscriminately in the art and entertainment of our time is to allow ourselves to be bombarded with telestial images and ideas—to become telestialized.

The real issue, then, is not how much evil we can tolerate, but how best can we fill our minds with celestial ideas and images. Our challenge is to look *honestly* at the true intent of any piece of music, judge its moral worth, and then, if it be found wanting, replace it with something better.

PART FOUR

The Music of Today

*There exists a vast mass
of love songs of the poets,
written in a fashion
entirely foreign to
the profession and name
of Christians.
They are the songs of men
ruled by passions,
and a great number of musicians,
corruptors of youth,
make them the concern of
their art and their industry.*

*Giovanni Pierluigi la Palestrina
About 1550 A.D.*

As society marches toward its last days, the conflict between good and evil intensifies. The gospel is spreading faster than ever before. We see more temples, more missionaries, more conversions, more nations opening to the gospel. Simultaneously, we see more sin, more pornography, more drugs, more violence, more broken homes, more immorality, and more degeneration of society in general. It should come as no surprise that the same elements found in society as a whole will be found in the art and entertainment media of our day.

The conflict has existed since the beginning of time. Over a hundred and fifty years ago, the great composer Felix Mendelssohn refused to write music for something he considered immoral—the opera *Fra Diavolo*. He wrote:

> *In this opera a young girl divests herself of her garments and sings a song to the effect that next day at this time she will be married. All this produces effect, but I have no music for such things. I consider it ignoble. So if the present epoch exacts this style and considers it indispensable, then I will write oratorios.*[1]

Each generation fights the battle with the weapons of its own time. Among the most powerful weapons of our times are the mass communications media—movies, television, radio, art, magazines, books, and records. Although the battle goes on in all types of music, many of the more esoteric forms are ignored by the majority of the world. The most influential music today is the popular music of the young people, and that is where we will focus our discussion. Because of new technologies developed in the past two or three decades, the music world of today is different than it has ever been in the past. There are special circumstances which apply to the music of today. Let's look at these first.

Chapter 1

New Technology

Any musical innovation is full of danger to the whole State ... when modes of music change, the fundamental laws of the State always change with them.

Plato

Music today is literally everywhere—living rooms, bedrooms, bathrooms, factories, markets, restaurants, airplanes, and elevators. And for those who must have it even out of doors, there are portable stereos which can be taken jogging, walking, horseback riding, backpacking, and mountain climbing. One set is even designed to fit on the back of a dog for those daily walks. We need never sit and ponder the Grand Canyon in silence again!

The ability to produce enough volume to physically impair hearing with music is another new technology. Without amplification, a symphony orchestra or choir could reach a peak volume of perhaps 110 decibels, but could only sustain it for a short time. Today, three electric guitarists with amplifiers can blast away at 125 decibels for hours on end.*

Volume intensifies the excitement of all music, but as anyone in the music business knows, it is a "hype." It covers up poor musicianship. When auditioning groups for recording, I would often say, "Okay, I know how loudly you can play, now let's hear how well you can play." In short, "volume covereth a multitude of sins."

---

*Decibels increase geometrically—125 are ten times as powerful as 115, one hundred times as powerful as 105, and one thousand times as powerful as 95.

The development of electronically synthesized music opens up a vast new sound resource. Virtually any sound, existent or imagined, can be created, distorted, or duplicated. The possibilities for new sounds are endless.

Multi-track recording enables a musician to record one instrument at a time so that one or a few can accomplish what it once took an orchestra to do. It also gives the musician the freedom to sit by himself in a studio, improvising and experimenting until he comes up with just the "right" sound. In effect, this has led to a new process of composition.

During the sixties, Motown Records discovered a process of recording which works well in their specialty—Black rhythm and blues. This label makes the rhythm, the "feel," superior to all other elements of music. Producers go into a studio with only a rhythm section and experiment with various rhythms until they come up with just the right "feel." Words, melodies, and harmonies, which might get in the way of the "feel" are added only after the right rhythm has been found. Beat is the master here—all other musical elements are introduced to serve it.

Another modern technique is that of laying in hidden messages through the use of sophisticated recording techniques. The Beatles experimented with this almost playfully in *Sgt. Pepper's Lonely Hearts Club Band*, and even on some earlier albums. They played tracks backwards, threw in random recordings of animal noises and sounds from radio and television, and recorded sounds at faster and slower speeds than the intended playback speed. When the rumor got out that the Beatles' albums had hidden messages, people began playing their records backwards and at slower speeds, claiming that they could hear "Paul is dead" and "I killed Paul" messages. Although it has never been positively determined whether or not this rumor was planted purposely to sell more albums, it did result in the sale of thousands of records.

Perhaps more devious is the classic Led Zeppelin hit, "Stairway to Heaven," which, when played backwards, clearly says "Here's to my sweet Satan." Other groups have recorded similar messages through backward masking.

Many people wonder what harm there can be in messages that are sung so unclearly (or so quickly or slowly) that the listener never realizes he is hearing the words. Although it has never been proven that the brain decodes backward messages, research has shown that some subliminal messages will be understood by the subconscious part of the brain.

In one experiment, clinical researchers in the fifties showed a drawing of a face to a group of test subjects. The sex of the face was vague. The researchers flashed male symbols before one section of the test audience at roughly one fortieth to one fiftieth of a second—so fast that no one realized that he had seen anything. Consciously, the subjects only perceived a flash on the screen, something quicker than the blink of an eye. When asked to identify the sex of the face, however, they identified it as male. Another group was shown the same face, but this time researchers flashed a female symbol. That audience identified the face as female.[2] This and many other tests convinced the researchers that the brain does register information that it is not consciously aware of. Researchers later flashed such words as "Eat Popcorn" and "Drink Coke" before a movie audience at a subliminal speed. Sales of soft drinks and popcorn increased.[3]

A few years ago the film *The Exorcist* gained the reputation of scaring the wits out of audiences, causing people to get sick in the aisles and run for the restrooms. A researcher found that at one point in the film, the Catholic priest's face was replaced by a two-frame clip of a full-screen death mask— "skin greasy white, the mouth a blood-red gash, the face surrounded by a white cowl or shroud." The researcher interviewed audiences leaving the film and found that only one third of the people recalled seeing the death mask. One third were unsure whether or not they had seen it, and one third claimed that they definitely did *not* see any such thing. However, the third who did not consciously see the death mask were the same third who had the most violent reaction to the film. "Perhaps strangely, the movie's strongest emotional impact was among the one third who repressed the perception and consciously believed they saw nothing."[4]

In the music world of today, many people claim that they never listen to the lyrics and that the messages never affect them. Research, however, shows that our brains are marvelously perceptive and pick up almost any message within sight or sound, whether we consciously admit to receiving it or not. The message is stored permanently in our brains, possibly affecting our moods and attitudes just as much as if we consciously chose to listen to it. With today's technology, many devious messages may be entering our brains while we claim that we only listen to "harmless" music.

Modern technology also makes it possible to electronically produce whole new visual and audio environments at concerts. Play and opera stage sets have always tried to create an atmosphere in which music could be performed, but today's technology allows concert planners to go far beyond previous attempts to manipulate audience emotions. Light shows, oil projections, strobe lights, electronic gadgetry, pyrotechnics, smoke bombs, on-stage fires and explosions, and pianos being lifted into the air to burst into flames—all these devices and others have been used to mold the audience into a unified mass. The consumption of drugs and alcohol by large segments of the audience—a fact at almost all big rock concerts in recent years—further empowers the performer to manipulate his or her audience.

Peer pressure on the young is another tool which can be used to exploit potential record buyers. Research shows that there is little peer pressure toward a particular style of music before the age of eight. To that age, children seem to enjoy ethnic, classical, and electronic music, all without discrimination. Shortly after reaching that age, however, a marked change occurs. Children now feel pressure to reject all music except rock. In the fourth grade and beyond, students will cover their ears, cringe, and look around to ascertain that sufficient numbers of peers are doing the same thing. The preferred music becomes rock.[5]

Music has always had great power to affect people's lives. With the new technologies available to those in the music industry today, that power has increased.

Chapter 2

Moral Music

Music is a moral law. It gives a soul to the universe, wings to the wind, flight to the imagination, a charm to sadness, gaiety and life to everything else.

Plato

U p to this point we have discussed the power of music and its possible moral influences in very general terms. It is now the time to become very specific—to name names and make quotations.

Let's begin with the positive side of popular music. Although some pop songs are clearly obscene, and even the most innocuous often focus our minds on the things of this world, there have been a few songs with positive, uplifting messages. The power of music to lock these songs into our long-term memories, to be repeated over and over in our minds, can only be deemed good.

In the mid-sixties, The Byrds recorded a hit song called "Turn, Turn, Turn" which paraphrased Ecclesiastes 3:1-8. During the abortion controversies of the early seventies, Seals and Crofts made a vigorous anti-abortion statement with their hit "Unborn Child":

> *Oh little baby, you'll never cry*
> *Nor will you hear a sweet lullaby*
> *Oh, unborn child, if you only knew*
> *Just what your mamma is plannin' to do*
> *You're still a-clinging to the tree of life*
> *But soon you'll be cut off before you get ripe*

75

Oh unborn child beginning to grow
Inside your momma, but you'll never know
Oh tiny bud that grows in the womb
Only to be crushed before you can bloom

Chorus:

Momma stop! Turn around, go back, think it over
Stop! Turn around, go back, think it over
Stop! Turn around, go back, think it over

Oh no, momma, just let it be
You'll never regret it, just wait and see
Think of all the great ones who gave everything
That we might have life here, please bear the pain.[6]

During those same years, Cat Stevens recorded the gentle, psalm-like hymn "Morning Has Broken":

Morning has broken
Like the first morning
Blackbird has spoken
Like the first bird
Praise for the singing
Praise for the morning
Praise for them springing
Fresh from the word

Sweet the rain's new fall
Sunlit from heaven
Like the first dew fall
On the first grass
Praise for the sweetness
Of the wet garden
Sprung in completeness
Where his feet pass

Mine is the sunlight
Mine is the morning
Born of the one light
Eden saw play
Praise with elation
Praise every morning
God's recreation
Of the new day.[7]

In 1980 a Christian pop singer, Paul Davis, made the charts with a song called "Do Right" which said in part:

We just can't keep on living to the limit
We just can't keep on ...
You've got to do right, do right
You've got to do right.[8]

Previously, Debbie Boone had refocused a standard love song, "You Light Up My Life," by publicly stating that she was singing it to the Savior.

In 1981 a song called simply "I Love You" praised married love:

And since I made you my wife
I never looked back
And, ooooh, I love you
And, ooooh, I need you...[9]

This song was so rare in the present market that the press called attention to this "hymn to monogamy" as something truly different. Perhaps the fact that they had to ask the composer what unique circumstances led to a song such as this is, in itself, a sad comment on our society's definition of "normal."

Harry Chapin's hit song, "Cat's in the Cradle" told the story of a saddened man who lived to regret that he never gave more of himself to his children. The words read as if they had been written for one of the Church-sponsored "Homefront" television spots.

It's refreshing to hear a few positive and moral pop songs sung about the parent-child relationship. Barry Manilow in "Ships" and Dan Fogelberg in "Leader of the Band" both sing of the love they wish they had shared with their fathers. Stevie Wonder's "Isn't She Lovely" is a love song to his daughter, and John Lennon's "Oh Beautiful Boy" is a love song to his son. It is sadly ironic that after the immense amount of negative influence John Lennon has had on so many young people over the years, he was killed just as he released an album which focused on a rededication to his wife and children, and his hopes for a positive, family-centered, drug-free future.

In May of 1982, two singles in the top twenty-five contained highly positive moral messages. Paul McCartney and Stevie Wonder's "Ebony and Ivory" expressed the hope that all people will learn to live in perfect harmony. "Chariots of Fire," although containing no lyrics, constantly brought to mind one of the most uplifting films of recent years.

Other songs have praised such laudable goals as peace, equality, sharing, and freedom although many of them have carried political overtones which some people find objectionable.

Let it be clear, however, that I am *not* condoning all of the music by these artists or the artists themselves. I am trying to point out that there have been some uplifting pop songs through the years. But let's be honest. One of the reasons these songs stand out is that they are so rare in the music business today. The vast majority of today's songs do not promote morality in any way.

As we begin discussing today's immoral music in specific terms, there is great danger. Some lyrics are too obscene to print, and by printing near-obscene lyrics, we give publicity to that which would best be forgotten. This may cause some to think and see evil where they previously saw none. Some minds may become focused on the very evil which they should avoid. We previously discussed the danger of presenting evil in an unbalanced way. In wrestling with this problem, I have come to understand how the prophet Jacob felt when he wrote:

> *It grieveth me that I must use so much boldness of speech concerning you, before your wives and your children, many of whose feelings are exceedingly tender and chaste and delicate before God (Jacob 2:7).*

Nevertheless, I know of no other way to awaken people to the fact that Satan is using much of today's music to preach blatantly degrading messages. Obscene lyrics find their way into Church dances and into the homes of Church members. Words we would never permit to be spoken or read in our homes are played, sung, and repeated dozens of times— merely because they are set to music.

While many songs are bad because they stress the trivial and selfish things of this world (such as fame, wealth, and cheap thrills), the most objectionable of all focus on four major areas of immorality: drugs, sex, violence, and satanism. I will discuss today's music according to these four classifications, ignoring such musical classifications as rock, country-western, jazz, classical, ragtime, new wave, big band, or any others. Most examples are taken from the rock field only because that happens to be what most young people today listen to.

Chapter 3

Drug
Music

B eer-drinking songs have been around for centuries. Country-western music has glamorized tobacco, beer, wine, and hard liquor for years. But in the mid-sixties, a new kind of song appeared. Mystical lyrics with obscure words sang of the pleasures of a different kind of artificial stimulant. Songs about illegal drugs from marijuana to LSD appeared on the pop charts.

At first, society would not tolerate an open endorsement of illegal drugs. Thus, in those early days, double entendre and hidden code words were used to spread the gospel of drug usage to an ever-growing underground. "White Rabbit" by the Jefferson Airplane was one of the earliest masterpieces of double entendre. While innocently telling adults that they were merely singing Disney-like words about Alice's wild adventures in Wonderland, they could repeat their drug message over the radio many times every day for months: "One pill makes you larger, and one pill makes you small... Feed your head!" Lead singer Grace Slick and others have since admitted to the real meanings of their songs, as well as their own drug usage at that time.

Although the Beatles' earliest albums were filled with the bubble-gum type of romantic lyrics, their lyrics gradually began to concern themselves less and less with teenage romance, and more and more with something strange and magical—drugs. The drug influence could be felt as early as their *Rubber Soul* and *Revolver* albums. *Sgt. Pepper's Lonely Hearts Club Band* was their drug-centered masterpiece. It declared that everyday life was hypocritical, deadly, and boring ("Getting Better," "She's Leaving Home," "Good Morning, Good Morning," "When I'm Sixty-Four," and "A Day in the Life"). The solution to such tedium, of course, was mysticism ("Within You, Without You"), sex ("Lovely Rita"), and most importantly, drugs ("I Get High With a Little Help From My Friends," "Lucy in the Sky with Diamonds," "Fixing a Hole," and "A Day in the Life" with its "I'd love to turn you on").

In their biographies and public statements, the Beatles have admitted to extensive drug use during this period in their lives. More recently, Paul McCartney was arrested in Japan and jailed for several days for possession of large amounts of marijuana. One researcher asks a critical question about the Beatles—exactly what was their contribution to western society? His answer:

> *The Beatles popularized and culturally legitimized hallucinatory drug usage among teen-agers throughout the world.*
>
> *Hallucinatory and addictive drugs had never before been a part of any society's main cultural value system. Even in places like Indochina, where the French legalized opium as a technique of population management and control, drugs were confined to a minority of users— usually the economically or politically disenfranchised. Certainly, drug usage had never before in the world's history been advertised heavily—as a record promotion technique—by popular music directed at adolescents.*[10]

To appreciate the influence of drugs in modern music, one need only consider the titles and lyrics of a few hits over the past two decades: "Acapulco Gold," "Eight Miles High," "Strawberry Fields Forever," "Snowblind," "Purple Haze," "Along Comes Mary," "Brown Sugar," "Bend Me, Shape Me," "Magic Carpet Ride," "Cocaine," "Mary Jane," "Pre Road Downs" ("Be sure to hide the roaches"), "Bicycle Race" ("You say coke, I say Cain"), "The Acid Queen," and "Late in the Evening" ("I stepped outside and smoked a J.").

Jim Morrison, leader of the Doors, was one of many to die at a very young age because of drug and alcohol abuse. His heavily drug-related music is making a comeback today in films. His biography became a best seller in 1981, and films and documentaries about him are presently being aired. The group's name and image was taken from Aldous Huxley's book, *The Doors of Perception*, in which the author commented:

> *For unrestricted use the West has permitted only alcohol and tobacco. All the other chemical Doors in the Wall are labeled Dope, and their unauthorized takers are Fiends.*

Morrison was a tormented genius (I.Q. 149). His lyrics were artistically superior to most others, but they concerned themselves almost exclusively with images of sex, drugs, and death (including oedipal fantasies of killing his father and raping his mother). While he reigned as the hottest teen idol in America, he was heavily into drugs himself:

> *He gobbled acid tabs like beer nuts—or aspirin for that's what they now looked like: early Owsley from San Francisco, the original 'white lightning', pure and cheap and ... clunk. And grass, of course—bags and bags of it from Mexico. And then the sugar cubes.*

One reviewer said: "The Beatles and the Stones are for

blowing your mind; the Doors are for afterwards, when your mind is already gone."[11]

Morrison's death followed the drug-related death of Jimi Hendrix and Janis Joplin. Others to die were Brian Jones of the Rolling Stones, Al Wilson of Canned Heat, Keith Moon of The Who, Robbie McIntosh of the Average White Band, Sid Vicious of the Sex Pistols, Tommy Bolin of Deep Purple, Lowell George of Little Feat, Gram Parsons and Gary Thain of Uriah Heep, not to mention the king himself—Elvis Presley.

Some groups build their entire name and image around illegal drugs. China White (cocaine) is the name of one LA rock group. Rush, the name of another popular group, is a term used to indicate a quick cocaine high. The Doobie Brothers got their name similarly: "We were sitting, passing around a joint—a doobie—so we called ourselves the Doobie Brothers."[12]

As one rock writer explained, "Drugs are a necessary ingredient for many rock musicians. It is almost impossible to sustain the frantic pace, ungodly hours, and inhuman energy without resorting to some kind of drug. The rock musician thrives on the periphery of that high and uses it as a crutch to hold his position and individuality." In the same article, a well-known rock manager frankly admitted, "No matter what anyone tells you, drugs will always be part of the rock scene."[13]

Chapter 4

Sex Songs

Give me some music; music, moody food of us that trade in love.

Shakespeare
Much Ado About Nothing *III, iii, 61*

W ARNING: The following chapter is X-rated, and should be offensive to all Latter-day Saints. I would not dare mention most of what follows, except that many of these records are heard in our own homes and church dances. It is time for us to wake up!

Recently, I received the following letter:

> *I thought you might be interested in an experience I had a few days ago. I was driving a station wagon full of our ward's 12- to 16-year olds to youth conference. Out of curiosity, I decided to let them have free reign of the radio to listen to whatever station they normally tune into. For a half hour or so I made mental notes about the records played.*
>
> *In the first song a popular soap opera star sang of his desires for his best friend's girlfriend, who spent her nights "loving him with that body." In the next song, several sisters sang of their desires for a man with a "gentle touch," who would "spend some time, not come and go in a heated rush." This was followed by a very catchy, upbeat tune in which the female singer suggested that the lovers "get animal." Next came a brand new hit in which the singer implied that cheating occasionally on his wife was just what every "average guy" does. His only*

regret was that he actually fell in love with "the other woman."

At last there was a break—an innocuous song praising the joys of the "Pac-Man" arcade computer game.

Then it was back to the same old theme. Mick Jagger and the Rolling Stones begged a girl to "start me up." Then a woman with a very sexy voice told her friend's boyfriend to "call me any time—satisfaction guaranteed." (By the end of the song, he calls.) Another tune praised a "super freaky" streetwalker who was definitely not "the kind you take home to your mother." The singer tells of his desire to sodomize her "every time we meet." The half hour finished with a rousing song in which the lead singer fantasized about undressing a centerfold model in a motel room.

This station was not an adult, or even college-age or punk-oriented FM station. It was the most popular AM station in town, known for playing what we used to call "bubble gum" or "teeny bopper" music—the station listened to by most of the twelve-year olds several hours every single day. Whereas similar themes are treated in plays, films, and novels (as bad as that might be), most adults usually experience a particular play, film, or novel only once. What particularly disturbed me about these songs was the fact that I knew the very young listened to them over and over and over, many times every day of the year.

Over seventy percent of all popular songs are about love. The dividing line between noble, uplifting "love" songs and degrading "lust" songs can be very subtle at times. At other times, the difference is woefully obvious.

Songs and poems of adultery and fornication are nothing

new. Every generation has had its fill of them. Anyone who indulges unrestrainedly in physical gratifications, however, gradually needs more and more thrills to keep his or her life exciting. Even standard sex songs lose their appeal after a while. Just as Olivia Newton-John's recent hit begins with "Let's get physical," and ends with "Let's get animal," so record producers have gradually added perversions to their traditional preoccupation with illicit sex in order to sell songs. Today, songs containing references to homosexuality, transvestism, sodomy, masturbation, sadomasochism, rape, prostitution, and venereal disease have all been added to the traditional menu of sexual immorality. (As if traditional sins were not bad enough!)

The biggest selling album in America in 1981 was R.E.O. Speedwagon's "Hi Infidelity." The sound may be middle-of-the-road rock, but the semi-nude woman on the cover and almost all the lyrics portray subtle and not-so-subtle images of infidelity.

Actually, R.E.O. Speedwagon is comparatively mild. Many groups use sex in a much more open way. The Ohio Players display nudity on every album cover to help sell records. Several groups base their name and image on sexually descriptive words. The most obvious is the Human Sexual Response, with songs such as "What Does Sex Mean to Me?" Cheap Trick bases its name on a euphemism for inexpensive prostitution. Circle Jerks, the name of a punk group, refers to masturbation. Steely Dan is a sexual device for women. AC/DC is an old euphemism for a bisexual, and Queen means homosexual.

US magazine described a recent AC/DC album as a:

> *Gritting, seething album that AC/DC fans will find essential! Even hard-rock haters may find it palatable,*

*thanks to its R-rated humor (one song deals with nothing
but the singer's testicles) and its wild exuberant energy.
Meanness oozes from both words and music ... and it's
romantic too—well, it is if you think a song called "Love at
First Feel" can be romantic.*[14]

Rolling Stone (a pro-rock magazine) has called Queen
"the first truly fascist rock band. The whole thing makes me
wonder why anyone would indulge these creeps and their
polluting ideas."[15] Queen band members seem to glory in
their decadent image. One says "I like strip clubs and strippers
and wild parties with naked women. Sounds wonderful. I'd
love to own a whorehouse. Really, seriously. What a
wonderful way to make a living."[16] One of their songs, "Tie
Your Mother Down," sings of one man's plans to seduce a
young girl:

*Your momma says you don't and your daddy says you
won't
And I'm boiling up inside
Ain't no way I'm gonna lose out this time
Tie your mother down
Lock your daddy out of doors ...
Take your little brother swimming with a brick ...
Give me all your love tonight.*[17]

Other groups and singers openly admit to sexual
deviation. David Bowie acknowledges that he is a bisexual,
and even Elton John has said, "There's nothing wrong with
going to bed with somebody of your own sex. I just think
people should be very free with sex—they should draw the
line at goats."[18] Many artists, from Keith Moon of The Who
to Alice Cooper to Mick Jagger, have performed in clothing
and make-up which connote sexual ambiguity.

To mention Mick Jagger and the Rolling Stones is to

mention perhaps the all-time champion of vice. Most groups seem tame compared to them. Advertisements for a recent album called *Sucking in the Seventies* featured a seductive girl sucking her thumb suggestively. A previous album called *Black and Blue* contained a poster of a scantily-clad, badly-bruised woman. Certain feminist groups marched in protest against another Stones album, *Some Girls*, which carried such songs as "When the Whip Comes Down" and "Beast of Burden." ("Am I rough enough?" its lyrics ask.) Another album cover featured a close-up of a male crotch in blue jeans with a zipper which could actually be unzipped! Yet the popularity of the Rolling Stones continues unabated as evidenced by their highly successful 1981 cross-country tour of America. In fact, in rock circles, the debate over the greatest rock group of all time usually comes down to three groups: the Beatles, the Rolling Stones, and The Who.

The Who, like the Beatles and the Rolling Stones, has been successful for more than fifteen years. In 1979 their enormous popularity led to a tragic incident in Cincinnati in which 18,000 fans tried to crowd into a concert hall and eleven young people died of suffocation. Six months later, group leader Peter Townshend commented on the incident in *Rolling Stone* magazine:

> *We're not going to let a little thing like this stop us . . . We had a tour to do. We're a rock 'n roll band. You know we don't ---- around, worrying about 11 people dying.*[19]

The Who made rock history by bringing out the first "rock opera" with their album *Tommy*. It tells the story of a baby who goes deaf, dumb, and blind after seeing his father murder his mother's lover. The group manages to refer to adultery, prostitution, drugs, child molestation, incest, murder, rape, brutality, homosexuality, and masturbation all within this one

album. A few lines from some of the songs should prove the
point:

> *You talk about your woman*
> *I wish you could see mine ...*
> *I can tell by the way she walks*
> *Everytime we start to shakin'*
> *The dumb begin to talk*
> ("Eyesight to the Blind")

> *But tied to that chair you won't go anywhere*
> *There's a lot I could do with a freak.*
> *How would you feel if I turned on the bath*
> *Ducked your head under and started to laugh.*
> ("Cousin Kevin")

> *Give us room and close the door*
> *Leave us for a while*
> *Yeah, your boy won't be a boy no more;*
> *Young, but not a child.*
> *I'm the gypsy—the acid queen.*
> *Pay before I start.*
> ("The Acid Queen")

> *We're not gonna take you!*
> *We forsake you!*
> *Gonna rape you!*
> ("We're Not Going to Take It")

> *Now I'm doing what I want to*
> *Fiddling about ...*
> *Down with your bedclothes*
> *Up with your nightshirt!*
> *Fiddle about*
> *Fiddle about!*
> ("Fiddle About"—sung to Tommy by his 'wicked Uncle
> Ernie')[20]

Perhaps the author of these lyrics (who admitted in a 1982 *Rolling Stone* interview that he had had several cases of VD) was speaking autobiographically when he wrote in another song in that same album, "Sickness will surely take the mind where minds can't usually go."

As a bishop, I was recently involved in a hot debate over whether or not the song "Whip It" should be played at a church dance. This debate, which focused on the double meaning of the song's title, became very intense. Some well-meaning young people insisted that there was no harm done as long as they didn't understand the second (immoral) meaning. In other words, "Unto the pure, all things are pure" (Titus 1:15).

I felt, however, that two other scriptures also applied to this discussion. In Matthew 10:16, the Savior told his disciples, "Behold, I send you forth as sheep in the midst of wolves: be ye therefore wise as serpents, and harmless as doves." Doctrine and Covenants 93:24 defines truth as "knowledge of things as they are." Living among wolves, we must be wise as serpents in seeing things as they really are. Some see evil where no evil is intended, and this is wrong. But others see good where evil clearly is intended, and this is equally wrong.

In applying these principles to the debate over "Whip It," and trying to learn the true intent of the song, we discussed the name of the group that had recorded it. The group is Devo, whose name signifies the "de-evolution" of mankind, the theory that mankind is going backwards. We also learned that the corporations which hold the copyrights to the song are called Virgin Music, Inc., and Nymph Music, Inc. Although the song had the supposed meaning of whipping a problem (as in "Whip Inflation Now"), it had a double meaning. "Whipping it" is also the common locker-room expression for masturbation:

> *When a problem comes along*
> *You must whip it.*
> *Before the cream sits out too long*
> *You must whip it.*
> *When something's going wrong*
> *You must whip it.*
> *Now whip it*
> *Into shape*
> *Shape it up*
> *Get straight...*
> *Whip it good.*[21]

Several of the older boys admitted that they knew what the song was really about and thought it a great joke to hear it played at church and school dances. Devo's later release "Jerkin' It Back and Forth" further demonstrates the group's fascination with hidden references to this particular practice. (Needless to say, in the aforementioned debate over the song, the bishop's will prevailed.)

Unfortunately, music is a way to let down one's healthy inhibitions. As one music scholar has noted:

> *Teenagers with guitar in hand will publicly express feelings toward the opposite sex which otherwise might not be expressed, at least in socially acceptable fashion. By serving as a means for expressing feelings toward subjects which are taboo, music allows the release of otherwise unexpressible thoughts and ideas and provides an opportunity to "let off steam" with respect to social issues.*[22]

In other words, music makes it possible to perform dance movements and say words which would be unacceptable if not

accompanied by music. It makes it possible to go beyond
normal restraints.

Thus Rod Stewart can openly invite a virgin to spend the
night with him in "Tonight's the Night," and even more
blatantly proclaims in another song:

If ya want my body
And ya think I'm sexy
Come on baby, let me know.[23]

Another group sings their hit "I want to kiss you all over," and
yet another belts out, "I just wanta make love to you." Oingo
Boingo has added its own dimension by singing, "I want to
make violent love to you!" And in "Never Say Never" Romeo
Void sings, "I might like you better if we slept together," amid
other unprintable lyrics. In early 1982, two versions of
"Johnny, Are You Queer?" were being sung on the radio. (In
this song a young woman taunts a young man to prove his
sexuality to her in bed.)

Ted Nugent, famed as the "motor city madman" and
"gunslinger guitarman," who performs in little more than a
loin cloth, has released an album cover which shows a girl's
fingers literally scratching through his skin. The title song,
"Cat Scratch Fever," is a lurid depiction of venereal disease:

Well, the first time that I got it
I was just ten years old
I got it from the kitty next door
I went to see the doctor and he gave me the cure
I think I got it some more.[24]

While it is good that Nugent does, at least, make public
statements against drug usage, his songs and image go to great
lengths to promote immorality of another sort.

Supertramp bases one of their songs on a boy who believes

he must have sex with a different woman every day to keep his youth. In "Goodbye Stranger," they sing:

> *I'm an early morning lover*
> *And I must be moving on...*
> *Good-bye Mary, good-bye Jane*
> *Will we ever meet again*
> *Feel no sorrow, feel no shame*
> *Come tomorrow, feel no pain.*[25]

Soft rock also has its share of erotic music. We've mentioned the soft rock sounds of Billy Joel in "Only the Good Die Young." Paul Simon sings of switching bed partners and using prostitutes in "Cecelia," "The Boxer," and other songs. Billy Paul sympathizes with adultery in "Me and Mrs. Jones." Bob Seger begs that:

> *Although your dreams don't include me...*
> *We've got tonight*
> *Forget tomorrow*
> *We've got tonight*
> *Why don't you stay.*[26]

His "Horizontal Bop" hit is nothing more than a description of an orgy. (The title refers to sexual intercourse.)
And many artists have sung:

> *I don't care what's wrong or right*
> *Help me make it through the night.*[27]

Female singers are no less obvious than men in making known exactly what they want. Olivia Newton-John tells her date:

> *I took you to an intimate restaurant*
> *Then to a suggestive movie*
> *There's nothing left to talk about*

Unless it's horizontally
Let's get physical.[28]

Juice Newton sings about spending the night with no strings attached:

If morning's echoes says we've sinned
Well, it was what I wanted now.[29]

The Pointer Sisters want a "slow man" with a "slow hand." Another bemoans the fact that "lovin' you both is breakin' all the rules." The records of Donna Summer (in the days before she was "born again") were called "vinyl aphrodisiacs." And Tony Tennille and Carly Simon seem to prefer the "it/that" songs: "Do That To Me One More Time," "You Never Done It Like That," and "Nobody Does It Better." Carly even has to remind us that "Daddy, I'm no virgin and I've already waited too long." (James Taylor echoes "She's no virgin" in the background.) A group called the Waitresses sing:

I know what boys like
I know what guys want
I make them want me
I like to tease them.[30]

The flip side is titled "No Guilt." A similar song talks about a "casual tease," and asks a boy to "talk dirty to me."

Other musical forms such as jazz and country-western are no less guilty than rock. In one jazz hit a woman begs, "Make love to me, baby." We can hear the Oakridge Boys tell us that "Lovin' both of you is like a ball and chain." Barbara Mandrell sings, "Married, but not to each other." Mac Davis croons, "Sure enough one plus one makes two/sure enough fun makin' love to you," as he sits google-eyed, repeating his girl friend's measurements. David Houston echoes Chicago's

"Motel Lover" idea in "No Tell Motel" ("We're here all night
... cheatin' has become our way of life.")

Other non-rock hits are called "Heaven Was a Drink of
Wine," "Heaven Is Just a Sin Away," "It's a Cheatin'
Situation," "Put Your Clothes Back On," "If Lovin' You Is
Wrong, I Don't Wanna Be Right," and "It Don't Feel Like
Sinnin' to Me."

Yet many people tell us that since some of these songs are
so well done there can be no harm in listening to them. We
need only look at the drastic changes in society in the last two
decades to see their influence. Sexual immorality and drug
usage have always gone on in secret, but they have never
before been the openly admitted and accepted norm of
American life. Yet within the last ten to twenty years, society's
values have changed to the point that all the former taboos are
considered light humor in most television shows and movies.
Without ever subjecting these vital issues to a rational debate,
many Americans have allowed their attitude toward sin to
change from hatred to endurance to pity, to embracing, all
within a ten- to fifteen-year period called by some "the sexual ⌐
revolution." Of the many factors which aided this revolution,
music has been a major one. In the words of Giorgio
Gomelsky, an early promoter and producer of the Rolling
Stones:

> *No one in their right mind would deny the lifestyle
> transformation that music brought about in our society.
> Take jazz or rock 'n roll. A form of artistic rebellion
> against the entrenched tastes of the establishment, and
> considered noise by the same ... our society has never been
> the same since.*[31]

As for the future, it may be safely said that although the
lyrics, the titles and the names of the groups will change from

month to month, illicit and immoral songs will continue to be made as long as they sell. Debbie Harry of Blondie summarizes the relationship between sex and song as well as anyone: "I've always thought that the main ingredients in rock are sex, really good stage shows, and really sassy music. Sex and sass, I really think that's where it's at."[32] And her lead guitarist agrees. "Everybody takes it for granted that rock and roll is synonymous with sex."[33]

Chapter 5

Music for Revolution, Violence, and Anarchy

*I knew a very wise man who believed that if a man were
permitted to make all the ballads, he need not care who
should make the laws of a nation.*

Andrew Fletcher, 1704

B ob Dylan was one of the first to give folk rock a heavy
political message:

*Don't criticize what you don't understand
Your sons and your daughters are gettin' out of hand...
The times, they are a changin'.*[34]

During those early years, musicians seemed to revel in
their chance to gain political influence. Graham Nash boasted
that "Pop music is the mass medium for conditioning the way
people think."[35] Mick Jaggar proclaimed, "We are moving
after the minds and so are most of the new groups."[36] Sid
Bernstein, who organized three early Beatle concerts, noted:
"Only Hitler ever duplicated their power over crowds. I am
convinced they could sway a presidential election if they
wanted to."[37] Although John Lennon sang at one time that
"you can count me out" of a revolution, and that "If you go
carryin' pictures of Chairman Mao/You ain't gonna make it
with anyone anyhow,"[38] he later made another version of the
same song in which he altered the lyrics to say, "you can count
me out, *and in* [the revolution]." In the early seventies, much
of his music took on an increasingly anti-religious and pro-
Marxist tone.

But I wonder if any of these earlier singers could have
guessed where their "revolution" would end up today. The

revolution of the sixties and seventies was based on a certain youthful idealism, at least, with ultimate goals of racial equality, peace, and love. That love soon turned into open sex, nudity, and drugs, and the peace became increasingly violent.

That same anti-establishment tone of those earlier days has experienced a recent rebirth in the musical styles of new wave and punk rock. Unfortunately, many of these groups, who seem to have the same violent tendencies as the previous generation, do not even pretend to have any of the ideals. Wearing T-shirts with "No Values" printed across them, they gather in concerts to do a dance called "The Slam" where they simply smash into each other with all their might. One LA nightclub serves its liquor in paper cups because it fears glasses might be used as weapons. Some of the more popular punk groups are called X, Fear, The Circle Jerks, China White, Black Flag, The Adolescents, Agent Orange, The Plimsouls, and Pil (Public Image, Ltd.).

Wendy O. Williams of the Plasmatics, "America's foremost sex-and-violence band," recently explained to Tom Snyder on network television why she destroyed television sets and automobiles on stage during her concerts. She claimed that she was making an antimaterialistic statement to America, asking why people got so upset over the destruction of a television set and ignored the murder and rape of human beings that goes on all around. However, to hear of her concerts where she makes lascivious gestures with her microphone stand, sprays four-letter obscenities on the cars on stage before she throws T.N.T. inside to explode them, chainsaws guitars in half, and removes her clothes to perform either topless or in a scant costume of shaving cream and leather, one might be led to wonder if this former performer in live sex shows is nothing more than an expert manipulator of the audience. She recently told a nationwide television audience:

> *Rock 'n roll has always been sexual. Rock 'n roll has always been violent. It has teeth. It will scratch your face off. That's why I like it ... If you like having your brains blown out and pushed up against the wall, then it's for you.*[39]

"Madman" Ted Nugent likes to taunt his audience with what he calls "combat rock." He claims, "rock is a perfect primal method of releasing our violent instincts. I used to rape [an audience], now I like a little foreplay. I literally demand a reaction from an audience."[40]

He likes to play his guitar as if it were a machine gun, but he recently received his comeuppance when auditioning an admiring guitar player who tried to imitate his machine-gun style. In the middle of a number sung to the tune of "Barbara Ann" called "Bomb Iran," the new guitar player suddenly pulled out a real machine gun and began blasting holes in the walls and ceiling.[41]

Hopefully, no group will go further than the punk rock group called The Dead Kennedys in advocating violence. Wearing costumes with "red rum" written across them (*murder* spelled backwards), they sing "I Kill Children":

> *God told me to skin you alive ...*
> *I kill children*
> *Like to watch them die*
> *I kill children*
> *Make their mommas cry*
> *Run them over with my car*
> *Like to hear them scream*
> *Feed them poison candy*
> *To spoil their Halloween!*[42]

Full-page ads have recently run in the rock trade papers

showing a gruesome corpse carrying a bloody axe, announcing the album "Iron Maidens" by Killers. "The Killers world tour '81," the ad reads, "has left audiences slaughtered in the aisles ... now the axe continues to fall on America!"

Alice Cooper is well-known for staging rock guillotine beheadings on stage, along with other macabre productions. Kiss, a group known to draw the youngest audiences in the business (many as young as eight or nine attend their concerts), dress up in evil-looking theatrical makeup and wear spikes on their gloves and clothes. At the Pink Floyd concert based on the group's *The Wall*, dozens of dark-hooded characters with scythes and balls and chains marched around the stage, slowly building a wall of styrofoam bricks. Periodically they chopped up baby dolls. As the band endlessly chanted, "We don't need no education," children came on stage to destroy school desks and mannequins of teachers. Finally the entire wall was blown apart as the concert's finale.

Van Halen has introduced what some call "power rock." Various album covers present the group smoking pot, one singer standing in a mock masturbatory stance, and people engaging in street brawls. Such songs as "Loss of Control," "Dirty Moves," "Mean Streets," "Push Comes to Shove," and "Running with the Devil" grace his albums entitled *Fair Warning* and *Women and Children First*.

A film about punk rock, *The Decline of Western Civilization*, is advertised with suggestions that you "see it in the theater—where you can't get hurt." Upon seeing it, actor John Voigt stated, "This reminds me of Germany before the Holocaust. That's how degenerate it is."[43]

Perhaps the greatest provoker to violence is John Lydon and PiL. (He was formerly called Johnny Rotten with the Sex Pistols.) One of his newest albums was acclaimed as "the most brutal, frightening music Lydon has lent his voice to since

'Anarchy in the U.K.'"[44]

At a recent concert at the Ritz in New York, the band refused to play in front of the audience, but instead appeared behind a large screen upon which huge images of them playing were projected. Lydon, however, refused to play the kind of rock 'n roll the audience had paid to listen to. "A drunk, sweaty, uncomfortable audience is a powder keg that Lydon, who always loves to play with matches, just can't resist and trouble flared up in short order." His unorthodox music was nothing more than a few splatters of drums with some guitar riffs thrown in—"dark, ominous, abrasive, primitive, and minimal. Done sloppily, it becomes noise."

Apparently they were sloppy that night because the audience grew more and more resentful of the "noise," and the band grew ever more aggressive. Lydon had the audience trapped—if they rejected him they were narrow-minded and intolerant, unable to understand new music, but if they accepted his sloppy performance, they were "mindless sheep," willing to applaud "the emperor's new clothes." They began to reject him by tossing jeers and beer bottles at the stage. One band member screamed tauntingly, "if you destroy this screen, you will be destroyed!" The jeers increased, and chairs and more beer bottles were thrown at the stage—some from the balconies. Several people were injured. When the band realized it was in physical danger, Lydon said, "I'm so glad you're open to new ideas," and fled the stage, just avoiding a riot.[45]

Purposeful violence and violent provocation are becoming almost the norm in the punk scene of today—a scene which boasts that it has "no values."

Chapter 6

Satanic Music

It sometimes appears as if Satan has brought up the top writers, musicians, and singers in our day to reign with blood and terror throughout the world. Some may think this is an overstatement and may be offended to hear their music labeled satanic, but let's look further. Moroni 7:17 tells us that anything which persuades us to do evil (such as the songs mentioned in the last three sections) is ultimately "of the devil." But, unfortunately, there are several groups which have progressed beyond merely trying to persuade us to do evil. By their own admission and boasting, many have become heavily involved in the occult, in witchcraft, in black magic, and in Satan worship itself. Such groups use their music and their lyrics to spread this mysticism and demonology to the public at large.

How could this happen? As we know, Satan is the master deceiver. Korihor confessed, "The devil hath deceived me; for he appeared unto me in the form of an angel" (Alma 30:52). Many people with good intentions find themselves serving the devil. Satan is always clever and subtle—at first. It is sometimes only with the clear vision of hindsight that we can discern where a certain path has been leading us. But the further we go down a path, the easier it should become to see where we are going. After one or two mistakes we should learn our lessons. As the recently "born again" early star of rock 'n roll, Little Richard, has testified:

> *I was making $10,000 an hour; sometimes $40,000, but I discovered what I never had with money, sex, and drugs: peace. People in rock 'n roll have good intentions, but I didn't realize I was working for the devil. Rock 'n roll clouds the senses and hypnotizes the brain.*[46]

Surely, many other "sincere" people have entered Satan's service unaware. But sincerity of belief is no guarantee of right belief or behavior. Adolph Hitler, Charles Manson, and Jim Jones probably all began as sincere men who thought they had only the best intentions for others. Somehow, they were deceived.

In the mid-sixties, Paul Revere and the Raiders tried to warn us that "kicks just keep getting harder to find." This may be the reason Satan is able to deceive so many. The deception comes on two fronts.

First, because financial rewards in the rock world are so great, competition is incredibly stiff. Hundreds of new records are released every month and very few of them are ever heard on the radio. As a result, many new groups will go to almost any length to stand out from the crowd. If talent won't gain the audience's attention, perhaps outrageousness will. Thus, with each successive year the temptation to do something outrageous becomes more overwhelming for new artists. The public itself must share part of the blame for supporting increasingly outrageous songs. When the audience is bored with love songs, it gets sex songs. When it demands further titillation, singing groups will move on to drugs, violence, and demonology.

Secondly, a young rock 'n roll star who suddenly finds himself with enough money and fame to live out almost any fantasy, will soon become jaded and demand new kicks. He, like the audience, may turn down the road which will lead to "normal" sex, "abnormal" sex, drugs, bestiality, violence, brutality, and finally to the source of all such "kicks"—Satan worship itself. As Nephi tried to tell us, "and thus the devil cheateth their souls, and leadeth them away carefully down to hell" (2 Nephi 28:21). Or, as Alice Cooper sings, "Welcome to My Nightmare."

The number of groups who openly admit to fascination with the occult and black magic, and who clutter their album covers with symbols of numerology, cultic religions, tarot cards, and satanism appears to be growing daily.

Some groups, such as King Crimson; Yes; Emerson, Lake, and Palmer; Blue Oyster Cult; Steely Dan; Earth, Wind and Fire; Rush; The Eagles; and Fleetwood Mac, merely dabble in mystical and cultic words and symbols.

The Eagles are a rather mellow, seemingly inoffensive group who constantly refer to demons and witches in their lyrics, from "Witchy Woman," to:

You've got your demons, you got desires
Well, I've got a few of my own . . .
I've been searching for the daughter of the devil himself.[47]

The group bases its titles, images, and philosophy on the writings of Carlos Castaneda, a popular anthropologist, whose study of southwestern Indian tribes led him to promote the hallucinatory drug peyote.

Earth, Wind, and Fire's albums use symbols of witchcraft and pyramid cult worship on their covers. Fleetwood Mac dedicated its hit "Rhiannon" to the Welsh witch, and singer Stevie Nicks, in concert, has dedicated certain songs to "all the witches in the world."[48] Emerson, Lake, and Palmer's "Brain Salad Surgery" album cover unfolds successively until the innermost fold reveals a devil. Rush uses the mystic pentangle and sacreligious imagery on several of their album covers. Similar images can be found in the albums of many of the other groups popular today.

Even mellow songs like "Dream Weaver" by Gary Wright carry messages of the occult:

Fly me high through the starry skies
Or maybe to an astral plane.[49]

A Paul Kantner song for Jefferson Starship, "Your Mind Has Left Your Body," has similar connotations. Seances, tarot cards, astrology, astral projection, and other out-of-body experiences are being sung about with increasing frequency today, and such subjects are ultimately demonic in origin.

While Kiss and Alice Cooper claim to be mere showmen, they nevertheless choose rather bizarre and satanic ways of entertaining an audience. Alice Cooper's very name, which he received during a seance, is supposedly that if a seventeenth-century witch. Both groups put on elaborately visual shows filled with extreme costumes and makeup, mock beheadings, snake entwinings, chopped-up dolls, fire breathing, and other gory spectacles. Cooper has slaughtered chickens and performed other sacrificial rites at his concerts. Unfortunately, other groups are even further into Satanism.

The Rolling Stones tried to copy the Beatles' *Sgt. Pepper's Lonely Hearts Club Band* success with their own fantasy-like album, in which they all appeared on the cover dressed as witches. The album was titled *Their Satanic Majesties Request.* One Richards-Jaggar composition is called "Sympathy for the Devil," and another is "Dancing with Mr. D." Another album was called *Goat's Head Soup* (the goat head is a common satanic image), and some of it was recorded at a Haitian voodoo ritual.

Over a decade ago, the Stones organized the Altamount

Concert which was attended by 300,000 people. They hired the Hell's Angels as bodyguards, and four people died during the concert. One of them was a young black man who was knifed to death at the foot of the stage by one of the bodyguards as the Stones sang "Sympathy for the Devil." This was all captured on a film called *Gimme Shelter*. At the trial the Hell's Angel was found not guilty, a verdict which *Rolling Stone* magazine justified, asking rhetorically, "How could one Hell's Angel be held more accountable than Mick Jagger for his incitement to Satanism?"[50]

If the previous groups are not offensive enough, several are involved in the occult even more deeply. The way in which Led Zeppelin allegedly used backward tracking to insert "Here's to my sweet Satan" onto its "Stairway to Heaven" song has already been mentioned. Most of the lyrics written by this group contain magical and occult images of one sort or another. They add to their mystique by naming their albums after a hit song which does not appear on the album (but usually comes out on the next one).

Jimmy Page, lead singer, runs his own black magic bookshop in London because, he claims, he could not find a really good collection in the entire city. He has bought the house of the infamous Aleister Crowley, a man famed in the annals of witchcraft, a man who was so proud of his magic, murder, and perversions that he renamed himself "The Beast 666." His most famous publication is *Magick in Theory and Practice*. Page is an avid follower of Crowley and says, "I do not worship the devil. But magic does intrigue me." He claims that his mansion is literally haunted.[51]

"Black Sabbath" has built its entire career on "Satan Rock," using the number 666 on their T-shirts and album covers and holding altar calls to Satan before some of their concerts. Their leader, Ozzy Osbourne, who now performs on his own, claims to have seen "The Exorcist" twenty-six times and says, "I don't know if I'm a medium for some outside force. Whatever it is, frankly, I hope it's not what I think—Satan."[52] His recently deceased guitarist had claimed that black magic held a much stronger "high" for him than the heaviest of drugs.

Osbourne recently criticized some of the new wave music, stating, "Some band's called itself the Dead Lennons... They'll have the Wounded Reagans next week. It's sick you know." To prove that he did, indeed, know the meaning of the word *sick*, Osbourne pulled a dove out of his pocket, chewed off its head, and spat the remains on the table at a CBS business meeting.[53] He uses crucifixes prominently on his album covers amid goats' heads and other satanic images.

Perhaps he has inspired another group called "666" whose first release was called "Vicarious Filii Dei"—"Alternative Sons of God." And Jim Dandy, lead singer of Black Oak Arkansas seems to have picked up Black Sabbath's idea of performing satanic altar calls, for at a recent concert, during the song "Too Hot to Stop," Dandy chanted "Natas" until the entire audience was chanting with him. "Natas" is "Satan" spelled backwards.

Perhaps the most offensive of all bands is AC/DC, an Australian group recently grown very popular. Like Black Sabbath, they consciously promote their satanic image. They are missionaries for their cause. On the cover of their *Highway to Hell* album, the lead singer even wears satanic horns and holds a demon's tail as if it is growing from his own body, while another singer wears a pentangle necklace and other occult jewelry. Among their recordings are "Hell Ain't a Bad Place to Be," "Dirty Deeds Done Dirt Cheap," "Overdose," "Problem Child," "If You Want Blood (You've Got It)," "Get It Hot," and "Shot Down in Flames." The lyrics to their hit "Highway to Hell" proclaim:

Hey Satan
Payin' my dues
Playin' in a rock band.
Hey momma
Look at me
I'm on the way to the promised land.
I'm on the highway to hell
Highway to hell
I'm on the highway to hell
Highway to hell...
Don't stop me.[54]

In another song, "Hell's Bells," the singer screams:

I've got my bell
Gonna take you to hell
I'm gonna get ya
Satan get ya
Hell's Bells
Hell's Bells
My temperature's hot.[55]

A recent book, *Drawing Down the Moon*, tells of the great resurgence of witchcraft in America in the last two decades. If all this seems far-fetched and irrelevant to the Latter-day Saint community, it is not. The Dell paperback, *Jay's Journal*, is a slightly dramatized account from an actual diary of a bright sixteen-year old seminary student living in a small Mormon town along the Wasatch front. The book tells how he and several LDS friends got involved with "O" (the occult) and began practicing black magic. He committed suicide and several of his friends died in freak accidents.

Although other examples could be given, it is not my

intention to dwell on such subjects. Many concerned people have spent countless hours listening to suspect albums backwards in order to discover secret satanic messages. Although it has never yet been proven scientifically that such messages can affect the brain or be understood by it, science may one day prove to us that the brain is much more susceptible to such subtleties than we now believe.

Nevertheless, in my opinion, secret backwards messages are much less important than blatant forward messages. What AC/DC, Led Zeppelin, Ozzy Osbourne, the Rolling Stones, and others preach in clear English, put on their album covers, and admit to in their printed interviews, is harmful enough all by itself. Judging from these printed admissions as well as album covers and lyrics, proselyting is going on all around us. Many rock groups of today no longer hide the fact that they know who the author of their success really is.

Chapter 7

The Deadliest War

The best sort of music is what it should be—sacred; the next best ... has fallen to the lot of the devil.
Coleridge

Whether we like it or not, we are at war! We are fighting a life-and-death battle for the human soul, and our enemies are Lucifer and his hosts. We will need all of our strength and courage because the foe is strong and the casualties are eternal. The battlefield is the birthplace of all human action—the mind.

Music is one of the adversary's deadliest weapons. Using it he creates sugar-coated poison that can slowly destroy all our brightest dreams and leave us spiritually dead. The irony is that we take this deadly thing voluntarily into our homes, schools, and churches. Some surround themselves with it twenty-four hours a day. We share it with our loved ones. We pay millions of dollars a year for the privilege of exposing ourselves to it. Like foolish Trojans, we open the gates of our strongholds and let the enemy in.

Some people think their minds are unconquerable fortresses into which they can allow all sorts of evil and destructive thoughts. One fifteen-year old girl told me, "I don't see any harm in listening to just one bad song. I don't notice the album covers, and I don't really listen to the lyrics. I don't do anything bad because of the songs. I just like the music." Many young people have told me much the same thing, and they all ask a valid question: Can just one "bad" song really hurt me? The answer is yes, it can!

When a person eats unhealthy food, he often senses very little immediate effect. Even some athletes claim that "junk foods" have no ill effect on them. In truth, however, our bodies are the sum total of the foods we have consumed, plus our inherited physical traits. Similarly, our minds are the sum total of our thoughts and experiences in this life plus our preexistent personalities. Physically speaking, we are what we feed our bodies. Spiritually speaking, we are what we feed our minds. We would be more healthy spiritually if we never consumed any evil. Every bit harms us.

We are living in a telestial world, complete with telestial arts and entertainment which can fill our minds with telestial images. Telestial images stimulate telestial thoughts which result in telestial behavior. The natural product of a telestial environment is a telestial person.

We do not reach either the celestial or the telestial kingdom in a single leap. We inch our way toward our final destination by thousands of seemingly insignificant decisions throughout our lives. Each telestial idea we feed upon stimulates a telestial desire—each celestial idea a celestial desire. Few people consciously decide to leave the Church. Thousands gradually begin to find pleasure in doing the things of the world until, eventually, they become unactive and redirect their lives along another path—a path which began with just one thought.

The Lord understands this and has therefore given us this sharp admonition: "Come ye out from the wicked and be ye separate, and touch not their unclean things" (Alma 5:57). I believe that much of today's music can be counted among these "unclean things."

And so the war rages on. We cannot avoid it. There are no safe sidelines from which to watch it. We must choose sides and fight as best we can. But we should understand that it is the deadliest war of all. In a physical war, we at least know when we've been wounded, maimed, or killed. But in spiritual battles, Satan's bullets come with their own novocaine. Each time we are hit we feel less pain. The more hits we take the more desensitized we become. With our spiritual life oozing out of us, we continue to proclaim, "But it doesn't really affect me!"

When we consider music's impact on us, and how many thousands of hours we listen to it throughout our lives, it seems wise to choose for ourselves and our families music which builds up our spiritual reserves rather than that which continually wears them down. The Lord has cautioned us: "Let virtue garnish thy thoughts unceasingly" (D&C 121:45). Accordingly, then, our abandonment of immoral music is only half the battle. Cultivating a taste for uplifting and encouraging music in our homes is the necessary other half.

Afterword

Music is the art of the prophets, the only art that can calm the agitations of the soul; it is one of the most delightful presents God has given us.

Martin Luther

Music belongs to heaven to cheer God, angels, and men.

Brigham Young

It is a testimony to the incredible power of music that Satan has chosen it as one of the principle weapons in his latter-day arsenal. But though Satan can use music, he did not create it, for he is a destroyer and not a creator. Music was given to us by our Father in Heaven, and it is a powerful force for good.

The scriptures testify time and again of the righteous power of music. The book of Job records that when the Lord laid the foundations of the earth, "The morning stars sang together, and all the sons of God shouted for joy" (Job 38:7).

"O sing unto the Lord a new song," the Psalmist said. "Sing unto the Lord all the earth" (Ps. 96:1).

"The Lord Jehovah is my strength and my song," said Isaiah (Isa. 12:2). And again, "Sing, O heavens; and be joyful, O earth; and break forth into singing, O mountains" (Isa. 49:13).

In a vision, Lehi saw God sitting upon his throne "surrounded by numberless concourses of angels in the attitude of singing and praising their God" (1 Ne. 1:8).

At the Last Supper, Christ and his disciples sang a hymn (See Matt. 26:30).

To Emma Smith, through her husband Joseph, the Lord said, "For my soul delighteth in the song of the heart; yea, the song of the righteous is a prayer unto me, and it shall be answered with a blessing upon their heads" (D&C 25:12).

And on the sacred night of the Savior's mortal birth, the hosts of heaven joined in an unforgettable chorus which has touched men's souls and softened their hearts down through the ages.

Music is clearly one of the great and holy gifts which our Father has given us for our blessing and joy. Satan, according to his nature, has labored to twist and corrupt this instrument of joy into an instrument of death. It is always his work to spoil that which is finest and trick us into turning our life-giving powers against ourselves. But though Satan can tempt us to misuse this gift, its power for good remains and will remain forever.

It is unfortunate that we have had to spend so many pages dwelling on the negative aspects of one of God's greatest gifts for the blessing of mankind. Now it is time to lift our eyes from the telestial uses of music and examine its celestial possibilities.

I have discussed how music affects the body, emotions, memory, and the words of a song. This ability to elicit a powerful physical response can be very helpful at home, especially on Saturday mornings when it's time for the family to do yard work. I like to awaken everyone with an up-tempo, rhythmical piece of music. This is one of the few times you will hear my teenage daughters say, "Turn down the music, Dad. It's too loud!"

On Sundays and other occasions when we wish to establish a reverent atmosphere, we have found that there is no quicker way to invite the Spirit of the Lord into our home than by playing or singing spiritually uplifting music.

And when it's time to calm the kids down and put them to bed, there's no greater blessing to the bleaguered parent than the good, old-fashioned lullaby. To this day, I cannot sing or hear the simple words "Go to sleep my baby/Close your sleepy eyes/The lady moon is watching/From out the dark blue skies" without reliving the tender, warm, secure feelings of my childhood. I knew my mother loved me because she sang me to sleep so many nights.

Music can also strengthen family traditions. I can smell turkey roasting without thinking of Thanksgiving dinner, but I can't hear two bars of the songs "Swing the Shining Sickle," or "We Gather Together" without being flooded by a lifetime of Thanksgiving memories. These songs were always part of our Thanksgiving celebrations and will always be associated with fond memories of family and holidays. Listening to uplifting music together can itself become a treasured family tradition. I firmly believe that a child who grows up appreciating the world's great music will find a steady diet of rock 'n roll boring.

Because it has such emotional power and is tied so closely to our memories, music is one of our greatest gospel teachers. Gospel truths taught with music are felt deeply, memorized easily, and repeated often. Furthermore, those truths will come instantly to mind whenever we hear the music associated with them. Primary songs, hymns, the emerging Mormon pop music, and serious sacred music not only provide an alternative to the telestial music of the world, but tend to focus the mind on celestial concepts and encourage celestial desires and behavior.

Music reaches its highest potential, however, when we use it to praise God, for words alone are often inadequate to express the depth of our feelings. The great Book of Mormon missionary Ammon, struggling with this problem, said: "Who can glory too much in the Lord? Yea, who can say too much of his great power, and of his mercy, and of his long-suffering towards the children of men? Behold, I say unto you, I cannot say the smallest part of what I feel" (Alma 26:16).

Music, the royal art medium of the emotions, sometimes gives expression to those deep feelings better than words. Spoken hallelujahs can never compare with those hallelujahs sung in the glorious chorus of Handel's *Messiah*. The emotional impact on the audience as it rises to its feet cannot be expressed in words. It can only be experienced.

After words are spoken and written, printed and typed, and our hearts still yearn to express more, it is then that music rises to fill the measure of its creation.

Questions and Answers

Question: My teenage children are already deeply involved in the most offensive sort of hard rock music. What can I do?

Answer: First, try to realize that most teenagers feel a great deal of peer pressure to be knowledgeable about the music scene—it answers some of their need for self-esteem and gives them the security that comes from being able to identify themselves with "the group." Many teenagers use rock music as an escape from fears, problems, feelings of inadequacy, or boredom. Perhaps what you are seeing is only a symptom of the real problem. If this is so, simply insisting on a change in your children's listening habits will not be enough. As a concerned parent, you should delve deeper to find the emotional or psychological motivations for their behavior.

The most important thing you can do is to keep the communication lines open with your children—this is much more important than any success you might have in changing their listening habits by being hard-nosed. Don't ruin your credibility with your children by attacking their music because it is ugly or offensive to you. Instead, discuss the moral issues unemotionally with them, giving them ample opportunity to express their opinions. I have found that most LDS teenagers are very sensible about the issue of rock music, if they are approached sensibly.

Hopefully, as you reason together, your teenagers will come to share your concerns about offensive rock music, and will be willing to moderate their listening habits. If not, remember to keep communicating.

Question: My son listens to the stereo at such a loud volume, I'm afraid that in addition to driving the rest of the family crazy, he may be damaging his hearing. Is this possible?

Answer: It's far more possible that your son is affecting the family's sanity than that he's affecting his hearing with loud volume. Even though the equipment used in recording studios and rock concerts can cause temporary or permanent hearing loss, very few of us have stereo equipment in our homes that is powerful enough or sophisticated enough to cause hearing loss.

Your son is responding to the "hype" of volume—it makes the music more intense and gives it greater emotional power. He is playing his favorite music as it was intended to be played—loudly.

However, there is another issue that should not be argued away, and that's the issue of common courtesy among family members. Set a standard of volume with your son that the family believes is reasonable, and hold him to it.

Question: I have always believed that loud, irreverent music is offensive to the Spirit, but how can I communicate this to my 14-year old daughter, who is "hooked" on rock music?

Answer: I, too, have always held that the Spirit does not abide where there is irreverence and loud, brash sounds such as those we hear in much hard rock music. However, communicating this notion to a young teenager will probably be difficult. Recognizing the presence of the Spirit and sensing its absence are, generally speaking, qualities of a spiritually mature person. As your daughter grows older and gains more experience in the gospel, she will probably discover this principle for herself, and will naturally want to "let go" of those habits and pasttimes that deprive her of the Spirit.

In the meantime, however, be patient but firm in communicating to her your own need for a serene atmosphere in your home. Set limits on the volume of your daughter's rock music, and counsel with her to establish a standard of music that is "bearable" for the entire family.

Question: What can LDS youth leaders do to insure reasonable standards in the music played at Church dances?

Answer: Some wards and stakes would like to have a certified list of "okay" music and an approved decibel level. Unfortunately, it's never going to be that easy. Leaders must use their own judgment in these matters and find their own means of enforcing the standards they set. (One stake has devised a decibel meter that automatically shuts off the band's equipment if the volume limit is exceeded!)

Probably the best way to control the music at a youth dance is to choose recorded music over live bands. One ward I know of has had great success using a committee of youth, headed by an adult advisor, to screen the records played at their dances. Let's face it, the teenagers are much more familiar with today's music than their adult leaders will ever be, and can be much more perceptive, at times, when it comes to recognizing inappropriate songs.

Question: What musical standards do you set in your own home?

Answer: All of our children who are old enough study music—either violin or piano. We enjoy singing together as a family, especially on holidays and special occasions, and feel that harmonizing as we sing actually helps us be a more harmonious family. Hopefully, these regular musical activities are giving our children the training they need to appreciate good music of all styles.

Since we have two teenagers and one pre-teenager, we often hear the strains of popular music in our home. We have chosen not to deny our teens access to their favorite radio stations, but we have established limits on their use of the radio. And as parents, we're gratified and relieved to see that, as a result of earlier training, our teens willingly turn off offensive music.

The stereo in our home belongs to the entire family; my wife and I have not surrendered it to our teenagers. We have tried to include many different types of music in the family record collection, and we take our turns, along with our children, in enjoying our favorites.

Question: How can I introduce my children to the world's great music if I'm a "music illiterate" myself?

Answer: Just as you don't have to be a mathematics professor to see that your children get a basic understanding of geometry in school, so you don't have to be a musician to see that your children get good musical training and are exposed to a variety of the world's great music.

If possible, provide your children with formal training on a musical instrument. Ask their music teacher or a friend or neighbor with musical training to write a list of popular classics you can make a part of the family's record collection. Children love music that tells a story such as *Peter and the Wolf* or *Swan Lake*. Take your children to local performances of the world's great music—they will particularly enjoy a concert featuring music they have already learned to appreciate with you at home.

Remember that the object is not to make musical geniuses of your children, but rather to enlarge their understanding and appreciation of good music.

Question: Is classical music more moral than popular music?

Answer: Not necessarily. One of the most popular and simplest songs in our Mormon culture is "I Am A Child of God," and yet I cannot think of a more moral statement in the musical world! It is difficult to talk about such generalities as "classical music" or "popular music," because there will always be that music which defies either category and that music which neatly fits in both.

Perhaps what you are sensing is the difference in purpose between the two. Classical music is usually more artistic, deeper, and often requires an intellectual participation on the part of the listener. Popular music is created primarily to entertain. It is easily understood, not usually very "cerebral," and if it is successful, makes an immediate impact on the listener. However, none of these qualities of either type of music is inseparably tied to morality. In fact, both types may conceivably be adapted to either a moral or an immoral purpose.

Because popular music is so much more accessible to the average person, it is more often abused by those seeking a quick buck or promoting an immoral philosphy. Of course, the other side of that same coin is that popular music can be the most successful means of directing a moral message to the greatest number of listeners.

Footnotes

Part One: Reflections of a Mormon in the Music Business

[1] Boyd K. Packer, "The Arts and the Spirit of the Lord," *Ensign*, August 1976, p. 61.

Part Two: The Power of Music

[1] Patricia Lynn Ryerson, *The Effects of Rhythm and Music on Learning and Performance of a Motor Task* (Master's Thesis, USC, 1971), pp. 10-27; R.W. Lunden, *An Objective Psychology of Music* (New York: Ronald Press Co., 1953), pp. 150-177, 304-319.

[2] Rudolf E. Radocy and J. David Boyle, *Psychological Foundations of Musical Behavior* (Springfield, Illinois: Charles C. Thomas, 1979), pp. 253-256.

[3] See Steven Halpern, *Tuning the Human Instrument: An Owner's Manual*, (Belmont, California: Spectrum Research Institute,1978).

[4] John Diamond, *Your Body Doesn't Lie* (New York: Warner Books, 1979), pp. 7-53, 151-181.

[5] H. R. Haweis, *Music and Morals* (London: W. H. Allen & Co., 1871), p. 22.

[6] John Lennon and Paul McCartney, "She Loves You," Copyight 1963-1964 Northern Songs, Ltd., London, England. All rights for the United States of America, its territories and possessions and Canada assigned to and controlled by GIL Music Corp., New York, New York.

Part Three: Some Moral Considerations

[1] Meredith Wilson, "Ya Got Trouble," Frank Music Co.

[2] Christmas Message of the First Presidency, 1912, in Davis Bitton, "These Licentious Days: Dancing Among the Mormons," *Sunstone* vol. II, no. 1, Spring 1977, p. 17.

[3] Caroline Eyring Miner and Edward L. Kimball, *Camilla: A Biography of Camilla Eyring Kimball* (Salt Lake City, Utah: Deseret Book, 1980), pp. 23, 43.

[4] Billy Joel, "Only the Good Die Young," Impulsive Music, Jericho, N.Y.

[5] Paul Stookey, James Mason, Dave Dixon, "I Dig Rock and Roll Music," Pepamar Music Corp., Los Angeles.

[6] Marvin Junior and Johnny Funches, "O What a Night," Conrad Music, N.Y.

[7] James Young and Dennis DeYoung, "Snowblind," published by Stygian songs, administered by Almo Music Corporation (ASCAP).

[8] Alexander Pope, Essay on Man, Epistle II, 217, in *Great Treasury of Western Thought*, p. 642.

[9] Haweis, pp. 45-46.

[10] *Ibid.*, p. 44.

[11] Kevin Cronin, "Keep On Loving You," copyright 1980 by Eel Pie Publishing Ltd., quoted in *Song Hits Special*, 1981.

Part Four: The Music of Today

[1] Haweis, p. 91.

[2] George S. Kelin et al, "Cognition Without Awareness: Subliminal Influences Upon Conscious Thought," *Journal of Abnormal and Social Psychology* 57 no. 3, November 1958, pp. 255-265; Joel Saegert, "Another Look at Subliminal Perception," *Journal of Advertising Research* 19 No. 1, February 1979, pp. 55-57.

[3] Del Hawkins, "The Effects of Subliminal Stimulation on

Drive Level and Brand Preference," *Journal of Marketing Research* VII August 1970, pp. 322-326; Joel Saegert, p. 55.

[4] Wilson Bryan Key, *Media Sexploitation* (New York: A Signet Book, New American Library, 1976), p. 103.

[5] Radocy and Boyle, p. 230.

[6] Bogan and Jim Seals, "Unborn Child," Dawnbreaker Music Corp.

[7] Eleanor Farjeon and Cat Stevens, "Morning Has Broken," Irving Music Corp., San Francisco, Ca.

[8] Paul Davis, "Do Right," Webb IV Music, Inc., N.Y.

[9] Derek Holt, "I Love You," Climax International.

[10] Key, p. 137.

[11] Jerry Hopkins and Daniel Sugarman, *No One Here Gets Out Alive* (New York: Warner Books, 1980), pp. 17, 70, 164.

[12] *Rolling Stone*, 4 January 1973, p. 16.

[13] *Circus*, 17 April 1979, p. 16.

[14] *Us*, 9 June 1981, p. 36.

[15] *Rolling Stone*, 11 June 1981, p. 43.

[16] *Ibid.*, p. 46.

[17] Brian May, "Tie Your Mother Down," Beechwood Music Corp., Hollywood, Ca.

[18] *Rolling Stone*, 7 October 1976, p. 17.

[19] Quoted in John G. Fuller, "Death at the Coliseum: The Night that Shook the World of Rock," *Families*, October 1981, p. 120.

[20] John Entwistle, "Cousin Kevin" and "Fiddle About," copyright 1969 New Ikon Ltd.; Pete Townshend, "Eyesight to the Blind," "The Acid Queen," "We're Not Going To Take It," copyright 1969, Fabulous Music Ltd.

[21] Mark Mothersbaugh and Gerald V. Casale, "Whip It," copyright 1980 by Virgin Music (Publishers) Ltd. and Devo Music. Controlled in the U.S.A. by Nymph Music, Inc. and Devo Music. (Unichappel Music, Inc., administrator).

[22] Radocy and Boyle, p. 165.

[23] Rod Stewart and Carmine Appice, "Do Ya Think I'm Sexy," Riva Music, Sherman Oaks, Ca.

[24] Ted Nugent, "Cat Scratch Fever," Magicland Music Corp., Hollywood, Ca.

[25] Davies and Hodgson, "Goodbye Stranger," Almo Music Co., Hollywood, Ca.

[26] Bob Seger, "We've Got Tonight," copyright 1976, Gear Publishing Company.

[27] Kris Kristofferson, "Help Me Make It Through the Night," Combine Music, Nashville, Tenn.

[28] Stephen A. Kipner and Terry Shaddick, "Let's Get Physical," copyright 1981, April Music Inc., Stephen A. Kipner Music and Terry Shaddick Music, N.Y.

[29] Chip Taylor, "Angel of the Morning," copyright 1967, Blackwood Music, Inc.

[30] Chris Butler, "I Know What the Boys Like," Mergovingian Music/CRI-CRI Music.

[31] Giorgio Gomelsky, "Change is the Only Constant," *Billboard*, 30 May 1981, p. 16.

[32] *Hit Parader*, September 1979, p. 31.

[33] *People*, 21 May 1979, p. 82.

[34] Bob Dylan, "Times They Are A-Changin'," published by M. Witmark and Sons (ASCAP).

[35] *Hit Parader Yearbook*, No. 6, 1967, p. 70.

[36] *Hit Parader*, January 1968, p. 10.

[37] *Time*, 22 September 1967, p. 61.

[38] John Lennon and Paul McCartney, "Revolution," Copyright 1968 Northern Songs, Ltd., London, England. All rights for the United States of America, its territories and possessions and Canada assigned to and controlled by GIL Music Corp., New York, New York.

[39] *Entertainment Tonight*, 9 January 1982.